Rightsizing

Effectively

An APPA
Task Force
Report

APPA
The Association of Higher Education Facilities Officers

Contents

Members of the Rightsizing Task Force

Frederick L. Klee, Chair
Director of Physical Facilities, Ursinus College, Collegeville, Pennsylvania

Scott Charmack
Associate Vice President, Physical Planning, California State University at Long Beach, Long Beach, California

Ronald T. Flinn
Assistant Vice President for Physical Plant, Michigan State University, East Lansing, Michigan

Dean H. Fredericks
Consultant, State University of New York System, and former Assistant Vice President for Facilities Management (retired), SUNY/Buffalo.

Edward Naretto
Director of Facility Services, California Polytechnic State University, San Luis Obispo, California

Joe Spoonemore
Director of Physical Plant, Washington State University, Pullman, Washington

Pieter J. van der Have
Director, Plant Operations, University of Utah, Salt Lake City, Utah

Acknowledgments

This book is the culmination of a two-year effort by APPA's Rightsizing Task Force, a project assigned by then APPA President Donald L. Mackel and continued by his successor, then President E. Diane Kerby. We thank Mackel, Kerby, and the Board of Directors for their insight into the needs and concerns regarding rightsizing, downsizing, and restructuring of higher education facilities operations.

The 1993 rightsizing survey and this publication could not have been accomplished without the leadership and passion of Frederick L. Klee of Ursinus College. As chair of the Rightsizing Task Force, Klee developed the survey, tabulated and analyzed its results, and organized the members of the task force in their preparation of the individual chapters within this report. He has also served as an ardent spokesperson on rightsizing issues through presentations and articles. APPA gives its heartfelt thanks to Klee for his many contributions to this important effort. We are also indebted to Carolyn Klee for database creation and management, and to Lisa Eberz, who assisted with data entry.

The members of the Rightsizing Task Force have had first-hand experience with rightsizing or restructuring at their own campuses, and they translated that experience into the valuable and practical chapters you'll find in this book. For their hard work, we thank Scott Charmack, California State University/Long Beach; Ronald T. Flinn, Michigan State University; Dean H. Fredericks, formerly of the State University of New York at Buffalo and now a private consultant; Ed Naretto, California Polytechnic State University; L. Joe Spoonemoore, Washington State University; and Pieter J. van der Have,

University of Utah. We also greatly appreciate the wise words provided in the foreword by Samuel H. Smith, president of Washington State University.

Several APPA staff members contributed to the success of this publication. Steve Glazner, Wayne Leroy, and Diana Tringali worked on early drafts of the rightsizing survey; Glazner also worked closely with the task force as it began to transform its findings and experiences into a workable publication. Special mention must go to Medea Ranck, who worked closely with the authors and provided substantive editing, rewriting, and structuring to these contents in order to provide a readable and useful report. In addition, she handled all production management and printing details for this book.

Drafts of this report received valuable critical review from three APPA members, whose comments made this report stronger. Thanks to Donald L. Mackel, University of New Mexico; H. Val Peterson, Arizona State University; and especially to Margaret P. Kinnaman, University of Maryland/Baltimore.

Finally, we would like to thank the nearly 400 facilities professionals who responded to the rightsizing survey, as well as the many who shared their specific circumstances in follow-up interviews with Dean Fredericks. Our hope is that the efforts and report of the APPA Rightsizing Task Force will help them and others plan for the many changes occurring within higher education today.

Foreword

Dr. Samuel H. Smith
President
Washington State University

Managing a business, an industry, a government, or a higher education institution during a period of budget growth is challenging, but those challenges are small compared to those faced during times of budget reductions.

Today's reduced financial support of public higher education from state and federal sources forces us to accommodate budget reductions that we would have considered totally incomprehensible and unmanageable just a few years ago.

These budget constraints come at a time when we are beset by exacerbating budgetary pressures, including maintenance intensive high-tech building systems, new restrictive codes, mandated programs, and aging facilities.

How do we compensate for declining governmental budget support, hold fast to the tenets of our mission statements, and stay on track with our strategic plan? One answer is to increase private support. We also must work with our staff, faculty, students, institutional governing board, alumni, and friends to hold true to our mission and prioritize our services. Through the rightsizing process we can meet expectations and, at the same time, plan for growth without sacrificing productivity.

Throughout this book you will be exposed to empirical observations and techniques utilized by higher education facilities officers practicing the rightsizing process. You may review the advantages of staff incentives, equipment upgrades, service level alternatives, services consolidation, automation, and outsourcing. Case studies offer you techniques adaptable to your institution. These techniques may be conveniently verified by contacting the authors—your peers. These tough times are not going to last forever. We must view today's financial tightening as a unique opportunity to consolidate, reorganize, and downsize as part of the process of rightsizing for the 21st century.

Rightsizing Effectively: An Introduction to the Issues

Edward Naretto

The massive layoffs and budget slashing that began in the corporate world in the 1980s is now in full force among institutions of higher education. Declines in funding from various sources along with increasing costs have drastically reduced the budgets of most colleges and universities.

As the effects of reduced funding trickle down to the facilities department, facilities officers have been forced to sharply reduce expenditures. While immediate cuts in services and staff might work as a temporary measure, these reductions will be self-destructive in the long run. As facilities customers become more dissatisfied with lower service levels, they may begin to question the value of maintaining in-house facilities services.

It is the intent of this book to encourage facilities managers to step back from the crisis and take a long, analytical look at their department's structure and procedures. In-depth self-evaluation and development of a mission will lead to goals that can then be used as a framework for making decisions on how the department will adapt to future budgetary changes.

The Survey Findings

In fall 1993, the APPA Rightsizing Task Force mailed approximately 1,500 surveys to APPA member schools. Approximately 388 institutions responded. While the number of responses precludes a detailed statistical analysis, the survey results clearly demonstrate that many facilities departments are being hit with severe, repetitive budget reductions.

The Rightsizing Task Force decided to analyze the survey data by looking at the internal and external factors affecting these departments, based on written survey comments. Survey respondents were contacted and asked to expand on their comments. This chapter will introduce and summarize the common themes in the survey responses and introduce some of the internal processes that can help facilities directors plan a rightsizing effort. These issues are discussed in detail throughout the book, and are especially relevant to the three case studies.

Mission Statement

The mission statement is important in any organization to provide both the in-house personnel and the customers with a clear understanding of the department's purpose; it is the cornerstone of any rightsizing effort. An institutional mission statement is especially helpful to subordinate departments when developing their own mission statements. Even if the institution does not have a mission statement, the facilities management department should bring together a team and develop its own departmental mission statement. Once the mission is established, it must be shared with all members of the campus community, particularly with the facilities personnel.

The next step is to have each area develop its own mission statement, again letting everyone know what the mission is by communicating it to personnel at meetings, in newsletters, by posting it on shop boards, and by daily contact with personnel. Many of the campuses that responded to the survey developed mission statements during the rightsizing process.

Morale of the Survivors

The effect on morale of the workforce prior to, during, and after any reduction of personnel can be catastrophic. This is particularly true for the survivors of rightsizing when no end to the process is in sight. Again, communication and staff inclusion to build trust within the workforce are the most commonly expressed concerns in the survey. The anxiety of not knowing, or the "why, what, where, and who syndrome," can paralyze a workforce.

To avoid rumors that add to the anxiety level, explain the reasons and objectives for the reductions to staff in regular, timely meetings. Supervisors and managers can help employees understand and communicate their fears during the reduction of workforce by remaining visible and accessible. Keeping a positive environment is critical to the morale of the survivors.

Staff input on the rightsizing process can immensely improve morale and trust. Managers must be receptive to everyone's ideas and not be patronizing—today's workforce is knowledgeable and can be a valuable part of the process of rightsizing.

Empowerment Paradigm

Many campuses mentioned the importance of soliciting help from front-line operating personnel in making decisions on how to reduce budgets. After all, these employees have been trained for their work and can, in most cases, make informed decisions. This paradigm shift of empowering staff can increase the efficiency and morale of employees by demonstrating that their knowledge and skills are respected and trusted. Moreover, it permits supervisors and managers to focus on more important functions and, as in many operations, allows more responsibilities to be assigned to each supervisor or manager.

Although some employees will assume that the extra responsibilities should be rewarded, in discussions with survey respondents, most front-line employees enjoy the new responsibility. Involving staff in decisions that affect them appears to be a logical solution.

Strategic Planning

Few higher education institutions had prior experience in planning a rightsizing process or in dealing with budget reductions of the magnitude of the past few years. The survey results demonstrated the importance of strategic planning to reduce the impact on campus, particularly on the employees who are at risk of layoffs. Planning anticipates budget reductions by keeping the staff small and using outsourcing for work that is seasonal or project related.

Developing a strategic plan requires input from the campus community and the in-house staff. The plan must be circulated to everyone and, if possible, the plan should be discussed in an open meeting with all employees. Each institution should develop a plan and be ready to implement it.

Adjusting Service Levels

The campus community typically expects a higher level of service than facilities departments can provide, even during good times. Rightsizing has brought another dimension to customer expectations. The survey respondents indicate a need to address the impact of modified service on the customer and facilities staff. The staff must know what level of service is expected from them, preferably in the form of a written document that can be distributed to in-house staff and the campus community. Again, a team of in-house staff and campus personnel should meet early on to address service levels and the priority of services desired by the campus. It is also recommended that a five-year history of budget and service level reductions be included in the written document. Staff morale can be greatly improved if everyone understands and acknowledges the need to change the services they provide. Communication up and down the administrative hierarchy is critical in addressing the service level that the campus expects.

Innovation

Rightsizing can and does have negative connotations, but there are also positive aspects to the process. The survey indicates that morale among in-house is staff is higher for campuses that allow innovation on a routine, day-to-day basis. Offering incentives to find new ways to perform work will encourage innovation. Work teams can determine the kinds of incentives the staff would like and how they should be awarded. The team approach can yield cost saving ideas that benefit everyone. This process should be written and communicated to all members of the facilities staff in regular meetings to keep interest high.

Allowing team participation and innovation will empower staff and build morale, resulting in happy, productive employees.

Training

The need for training for many areas is mentioned often in the survey. Training for team-building, technical, and people skills, self-help programs, rightsizing training skills, and other areas are necessary for efficient operation. Some campuses use outside firms, other campuses prefer to use their own staff for training. Either in-house or external professionals (or a combination) can be used, provided the staff has input in the outcomes of the process. Off-site training can be used to build the trust component with front-line staff and is often helpful in team building. Campus follow-up on training must be immediate to keep staff enthusiastic and motivated about the training they have received.

Rightsizing training is an oxymoron; each campus has unique issues and processes, and all the training in the world cannot resolve budget cuts to everyone's satisfaction. The survey was especially helpful to understanding the processes that many campuses have gone through and provides direction in how to proceed when rightsizing is necessary.

Productivity and Efficiency Enhancement

State-of-the-art equipment, materials, and supplies are absolutely necessary to make employees as efficient as possible. There are many labor-saving devices that increase productivity and morale if the employees are involved with the process of selecting them. All materials, supplies, and equipment must be of the highest quality whenever possible. Third-party warehousing can reduce inventories, thus reducing funds that are tied up in inventory. Survey respondents remarked that it is important to keep up with new products and methods to provide the best maintenance service for the dollars spent. Beware of existing and new equipment that is inefficient or does not provide any benefit to the staff or campus community.

Busywork and multiple approval signatures should be closely reviewed. Many times staff do not have the ability or the training to effectively use complicated systems. Keep procedures simple, or at least within the capability of the staff.

Respondents stress the importance of maintaining quality, which must not be forgotten when rightsizing occurs.

Many product shows are held close to college campuses. Send the most qualified person staff; he or she can report back to other employees on new processes to make operations more efficient. Educational programs and professional association meetings can help employees become more productive and efficient. Employees will also meet colleagues through these programs whom they can turn to for assistance in the future. Our employees must become more productive if rightsizing and customer satisfaction are our goals.

Conclusion

No two campuses are alike; size, types of facilities, academic emphases, political structure, and other aspects vary. So it is with rightsizing. The makeup of each institution will intimately affect how each campus deals with budget reductions. No single cookie-cutter approach exists; however, using the general concepts provided here and the specific examples provided by the case studies and other chapters in this book can help facilities managers organize and plan their rightsizing efforts. It is the hope of the task force that the information contained in these pages simplifies the Herculean, but immensely valuable, challenge of rightsizing.

Findings of the Rightsizing Survey

Dean H. Fredericks

During 1993, APPA: The Association of Higher Education Facilities Officers surveyed its members to obtain answers to specific questions about rightsizing processes at their respective institutions. Three hundred-eighty-eight institutions responded, representing all regions of the country and, more important, an adequate mix of large and small, and public and private institutions. While the statistical data (results of the survey appear in the Appendix) revealed few surprises, the written comments appended to the survey indicated just how concerned facilities administrators are with the continual erosion of resources. Two hundred-forty (nearly two-thirds of respondents) took the time to provide helpful comments. These comments graphically illustrated conditions the statistical results only hinted at. Because this portion of the survey proved so interesting, follow-up interviews were conducted with many of the respondents, and four of those interviews are included as representative case studies at the end of this chapter.

How Common is Rightsizing?

The responses confirmed that, over the past three years, the majority of institutions experienced either no growth in their

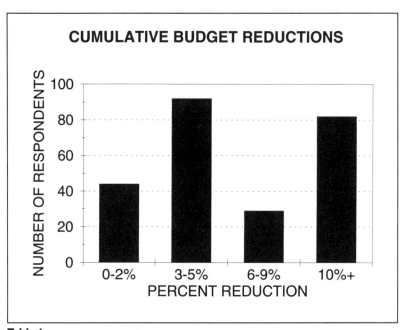

Table 1.
Budget reductions reported by survey respondents.

budgets or, more commonly, a decrease. Some public institutions suffered from mandated (state) decrees that came after
the schools had prepared preliminary budget plans in accordance with state budget targets. Typically these "final" budgets
are approved by the legislature and are implemented prior to
the next academic year.[1]

These last-minute cuts leave little time or opportunity for an
institution to be innovative, thus leaving the facilities budget
as the easiest target due to its large size and visibility. After the
task force reviewed all the survey responses, we concluded that
nearly every facilities manager has experienced some form of
rightsizing, and many apparently have had to yield to that
painful process more than once. (See Case Study 1 on page 24.)

Traditionally, facilities budgets are the first, and often, the
most deeply cut when resources are tight. As Table 1 indicates,
the majority of those surveyed reported budget cuts from 2 to
10 percent in the facilities units; 25 percent of respondents
reported cuts over 10 percent.

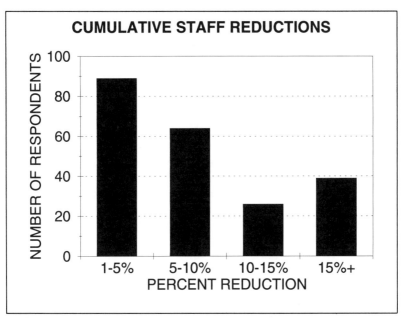

Table 2.
Cumulative staff reductions.

Labor absorbed the greatest reductions, with a majority of respondents showing up to a 15 percent loss in staff (see Table 2). Fortunately for the individuals involved, nearly all of those staff reductions were accomplished through attrition, although several state-supported institutions did report significant lay-offs.

Attrition, however, does not always correlate with institutional needs. All too often, those who leave are the persons with the longest service to, and knowledge about, the institution. Relying on reduction through attrition may mean that customers have to wait longer for services not only because there are fewer staff, but also because those who remain lack experience.

On the plus side, in the more technical areas and professional ranks, rightsizing in the private sector has resulted in a potential pool of extremely well qualified individuals who may be willing to start for salaries below those who retired from the institution, as is discussed in Case Study 3 on page 26. That example also includes reference to custodial rightsizing, which is explored elsewhere in this book.

The Impact of Rightsizing

The facilities areas most frequently affected by rightsizing are, as suspected, custodial and grounds. These areas are probably chosen because they consist of mostly entry-level positions, and as such, experience more turnover. Also, these areas may be perceived as "extras" by campus administrators who still believe in the old adage that "students can learn regardless of the length of the grass or the cleanliness of their classrooms." As most facilities administrators now know, this belief was clearly rejected by the Carnegie Foundation for the Advancement of Teaching in their report, discussed in Ernest L. Boyer's book, *College: The Undergraduate Experience in America* (1987), which clearly demonstrates the importance of campus appearance to recruitment. Many of the survey respondents too expressed this concern.

> *As we compete for fewer students with other institutions, as physical plant we must continue to maintain our campus. This is understood by the whole community. My concern is that expectations are rising while resources are falling.*

Others mentioned similar concerns:

> *[Campus appearance] will affect student recruitment; student education (not having the latest technology); and replacement building costs are skyrocketing.*

> *Quality education requires quality facilities.*

> *Ability to provide a quality environment for teaching and research is directly related to the funding available to physical plant.*

Fortunately, in recent years the quality of student life has become a primary concern for many high-level administrators. Interestingly, when shown as a percentage in Table 3, the areas hardest hit within facilities appear to be the paint shops, with losses up to 30 percent. This may be due in part to the typically small number of employees in the paint shops. Nevertheless, discussions with a number of facilities managers suggest that such decisions may have been based in part on the frequency of criticism about these shops' productivity. Several respondents indicated that they had cut the paint shops personnel to the point where they now paint only public spaces, and then only on extended frequencies. One individual at a large university stated the department painted only ornamental metal

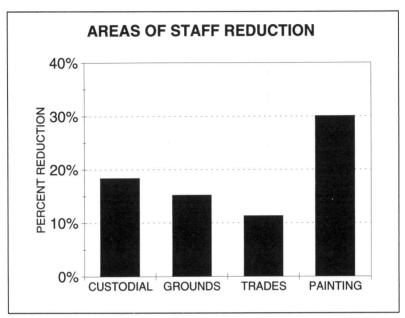

AREAS OF STAFF REDUCTION

Table 3.
Percentages of staff reduction by area.

railings, and with one painter! Student help and contract services have likely replaced some of those staff.

As indicated in Table 4, in addition to leaving staff positions unfilled, institutions are also purchasing fewer supplies and reducing levels of service as methods of cost reductions; we will discuss some of these strategies a little later in this chapter.

While reductions are expected to have a negative long-term effect on facilities, over half of respondents stated that the retrenchment efforts would have only a minor impact on the academic program of the school. That does not suggest that respondents are complacent and merely continuing to do "business as usual." To the contrary, the vast majority expressed concern over the eventual consequences of deferred maintenance. One respondent commented,

I have not had a reduction because all [meaning trustees, faculty, administration] agree plant is in poor shape. We have under-funded maintenance for more than 20 years.

It should be noted at this point that the rightsizing process did, in fact, enable some departments to eliminate tasks that probably should have been examined years ago. The following response captures well the driving force behind rightsizing.

Belief by administration that over time all departments develop some fat which could be pared with a good look at our own operations [while] still keep[ing] service at its present level.

There is little question that the sixties led to the promulgation of practices that were more like amenities than necessities. In his keynote speech at the 1993 APPA annual meeting, Dr. Keith Lovin, president of Maryville University in St. Louis, Missouri, conceded that times are tough in colleges and universities, especially within the facilities areas. He then startled the audience by concluding that "times are actually favorable" because we have never before had such great opportunities as we now have to cut or reduce operations that we consider not cost effective. Several members must have agreed with Dr. Lovin. One respondent stated

I believe this can be a healthy process, but it must be institution-wide and should identify and then concentrate on those few things we do well—we need to stop trying to do everything and stop trying (as an institution) to be all things to all people.

I am confident many of us would agree with the following:

The academic community as a whole does not approach cost-cutting in a business sense, they just react....For example, proper...scheduling of classes and use of buildings to reduce costs.

Many respondents concluded that the service areas, particularly facilities, are unfairly targeted, while academic programs remain untouched. One respondent wrote, "Are you kidding? We usually double the academic offering."

Others were not quite so emphatic, but still thought that other areas should be examined during the rightsizing process. For example,

Needs to be institution-wide. All areas participating. All areas need review, especially travel, membership, and computer needs.

All sectors [should] participate and take prorata reductions however possible. Also primary focus on service to students and consideration to employees.

That the established percentage of reduction be applied equally to all operating and academic departments.

However, the survey results confirm that, as the fiscal condition of the institution worsens, other administrative units and even faculty experience reductions. Nearly half of those responding—157—stated that other administrative units had experienced the same or greater percentage of reduction, while 25 percent indicated that the academic units were involved. Student life and residential services departments were reported to have also suffered budget cuts; however, these figures may be somewhat influenced by how these budgets are treated. At some state-supported institutions these budgets are considered "self-sufficient," and therefore dependent upon the number of students living in the facilities, rather than the fiscal condition of the institution.

A response from another institution suggested that "Restructuring, although painful, is a logical and healthy process. Helps focus on important goals."

The Role of the Facilities Officer

Changing past practices, however, is difficult to achieve without significant justification. Interestingly, respondents did report that faculty appeared to have greater empathy for the plight of the facilities units when facing possible reductions in their own departments. One member indicated that "at our institution, faculty were so concerned about the institution's fiscal crisis that they did not want to be identified as a complainer."

The vice president of administration at a mid-Atlantic state community college provided an interesting scenario, described in Case Study 2.

Many other members suggested (or wished for) the opportunity to participate in the initial discussions relating to budget cuts, rather than merely responding to a decree to cut their staff and budgets by some arbitrary percentage:

Institute real programmatic change; across-the-board-cuts are often ineffective and can be harmful.

There is no question that a budget committee consisting of faculty, when examining all budget areas, might be struck by the magnitude of the facilities budget, particularly should utilities be included in that allocation.

If the facilities administrator has earned any credibility within the institution, however, there should be evidence of prudent budget control, most likely in response to the energy crisis and, more recently, federal and state mandates.

Energy conservation and PM programs started several years ago gave us the slack required to cover budget cuts and freezes over the last three years despite square footage increases.

Nevertheless, funding for preventive maintenance and conservation efforts are among the first to be considered as "unnecessary" when funding becomes constrained. For these and other reasons, many indicated the need for additional input *before* the budget ax falls.

Physical plant administration must be included in decision making! Probably a small college concern.

While there is certainly truth in that recommendation, clearly it is not merely a small college concern. In fact, large public institutions may be even more tempted to make cuts predicated more on dollars than needs. Those sentiments are expressed as follows:

No involvement from affected groups.

Physical plant department should have some input.

Out of sight—out of mind mentality toward maintenance budgets is dangerous, considering the level of deferred maintenance.

Ensure that the physical plant director is involved in the restructuring and long-range planning.

Facilities managers need to be included at a level of input in order to make a case for shared reductions. Too often we are advised after-the-fact of our situation, leaving us in a reactive posture, not a productive position of management.

Not everyone has been excluded from the process, however. One facilities administrator at a state university actually volunteered to serve on that institution's task force for reallocation. He stated that he found that experience, while time-consuming, to be invaluable. Working elbow-to-elbow with the deans and faculty taught him a lot about the academic priorities at that institution, even though he had been there for many years. Even more important, he taught others on the task force about the facilities requirements. He admitted that he "got political" and the task force actually recommended that the facilities budget be increased. While that recommendation was overruled at a higher level, he was able to protect his budget when the "less political" could not.

Another respondent echoed those thoughts, suggesting "Cultivate a professional relationship with the budget director and emphasize the cost of facilities management."

Even if one is fortunate enough to participate in the institutional budget (reallocation) process, to assume that the facilities budget will escape any reduction in resources is probably naive. There are few facilities administrators indeed, who do not understand the rationale for "rightsizing" service areas early in the restructuring process, nor do they initially question why facilities areas are often the first targeted. The best that can be anticipated is the slowing of the gradual erosion of base funding. And, even though faculty are often involved in the decision making, they will still complain about a lack of services, regardless of the cause. To quote another respondent,

Service expectations are not downgraded with restructuring. Everyone expects the same or better service with fewer people.

Documentation is an important tool in any budget negotiations. One respondent was experiencing significant erosion of facilities resources under one administration, but continued to document the growing list of deferred projects. When a new administration eventually took control, the erosion was recognized and the trustees supported a major increase in funding for deferred maintenance.

Preparing an audit and demonstrating the consequences can be an effective method for educating the institution on facilities needs. One respondent explained that, while the department had always maintained a "list of needs" and requested funding each year for those with the highest priority, they never had the "big list"—a comprehensive listing that demonstrated just how much could or should be completed. While it took time to audit each facility and generate a list, he learned that with the "big list" of deferred maintenance items, his administration and the trustees were much less likely to reduce his annual funding.

Zero-base budgeting may seem somewhat mysterious to some facilities administrators. This may be particularly true in some state institutions where, at least in the past, administrators could always assume at least the same base budget, adjusted to reflect new or increased needs such as inflationary increases. That has all changed, but too few facilities managers have taken the time to develop a zero-base budget to show the costs for every level of service.

Service departments [must] quantify their services/service levels to allow adjustments per plan, not just percentage across-the-board reduction.

Assuming that reductions must occur, the next logical question is where and how to make those changes. One might be tempted, after repeated cuts in the budget, to become vindictive and, as so often occurs in local municipality and school district budgets, "hit them where it hurts most," and hope public opinion will sway mandated cuts. After all, the facilities budgets are seldom self-serving. Most expenditures directly support other academic functions, including the largest budget area: utilities. Even the most innovative conservation programs depend heavily on support from the entire institutional community. Some facilities budgets have included mandated savings in energy consumption. One response identified the ideal process:

Reductions should be made by consensus regarding the level of service required or desired—not punitive (i.e., don't reduce certain budgets to get back at someone).

In other words, service levels must be examined and some rational approach determined for how the facilities department should respond to mandated cuts. Several institutions have successfully attempted to quantify their services. Ron Flinn provides interesting insights into his efforts at Michigan State University elsewhere in this book. Case Study 4 provides a look at similar efforts at another large institution.

Such was also the case at my former institution, a large public university. While we kept good records and charged all expenditures against categories as listed in the state finance bulletin, the categories were rather broad: custodial, grounds, structural repairs, and mechanical systems. And, even though we had a good work order system that categorized work by shop (even down to the type of work, such as door repairs, vandalism repair, broken plumbing fixtures), the two systems did not "talk to each other." At that time, only recoverable charges (labor and material) were fully "costed"; additional information, such as material quantities and number of labor hours was certainly available, but not recorded or summarized. It merely stayed with the completed work order. Therefore, we could not easily determine total costs by shop, as reconciled with our institutional budget. Further, major service contracts for trash removal, elevator maintenance, environmental controls, etc., were controlled by our maintenance operations center, and therefore "charged" against an administration account.

In an effort to demonstrate to our budget committee just where our money was being spent, I initiated a process to develop costs per shop. Although I had been on the campus for over 18 years and thought I knew my operations, I found this exercise to be very interesting, albeit very time consuming. The institution was a two-campus operation and the newer, all-electric campus, started in 1973, had grown to over 4 million OGSF (outside gross square feet) in a little over fifteen years. The older campus was heated by a central coal-fired plant. The newer campus had mostly drywall partitions; the older utilized masonry construction. As with any "benchmarking" exercise, I needed to demonstrate the differences between the campuses in order to show the administration why our costs per category and shops varied between campuses.

Yes, there were some who suggested we use the shop with the lowest costs per square foot and dissolve the other. By graphically comparing such things as the costs per square foot per campus and comparisons with previous years, we could demonstrate our effectiveness in managing our resources. In fact, at the budget presentation to our vice president, those present agreed that some of our funding should be restored. Shortly thereafter, one of those mid-year "adjustments" required deeper than anticipated cuts in the institution's resources; however, our budget remained untouched.

In any situation, the following principle applies: the purpose of higher education is to instruct, not to administer, so support units must take cuts to help with instruction.

As mentioned earlier, participation in the overall budget process provides greater insight into the institution's long-range planning process. At the very least, facilities managers should have an understanding of the institutional mission statement and their relationship to that overall mission.

Facilities are usually not participants in strategic plan development; yet they contribute in great measure, in both dollars and personnel, to retrenchment and solutions.

I have suggested in this chapter that budget cuts have been common for many of us for many years. While many of us continue to hope better days are coming, realistically we should begin to develop a long-range planning process.

Most institutions have a mission statement, as do many physical plant organizations. In the former, the differences typically reflect the size and type of institution and the specialization of same. Mission statements for the latter, however, are usually generic, and reference the institutional mission with a few facilities "buzzwords." (See Frederick Klee's chapter on strategic planning for information on developing a departmental mission statement.)

Institutional mission statements must, however, consider the impact upon the facilities department. One survey respondent recalled a speech by the newly arrived president at his school, a large state institution, who proudly proclaimed that the institutional mission would focus on increased research (grant) funding, achieving Division I athletic status, and increased attention to and support for community development (town and gown activities).

One can easily envision the dilemma that caused for the facilities administrator. Three major constituencies, under three separate vice presidents, now believed they were number one! And, the facilities budget did not increase, but rather, maintenance positions and supply budgets were "frozen," despite inflationary increases.

The "we are number one" complex was so compelling that one faculty person suggested to the president that the type (hardness) of pencils supplied by the central stores be changed so that the inscription on them would read "State University #1."

One cannot deny that facilities (size, number, quality) affect everyone in the academic/research community. Therefore, one might properly question the notion of restructuring facilities without first defining the eventual structure (mission and strategic plan) of the institution as a whole. Structuring should be based on the institutional needs as opposed to individual needs.

Typically, facilities are physically renovated to better suit their proposed use. Using this principle, would it not therefore be proper to delay the downsizing of the facilities units pending a revised definition of the institution's mission so the two are complementary? One respondent had that same thought:

> *The facility cuts should take place after, and not concurrent with, the academic and research units in order to strategically cut services coincident to [the] university thrust and mission.*

Nevertheless, the converse is more often the norm. Another very troublesome aspect of the rightsizing process, particularly in public institutions, is the absence of long-range planning. In fact, many institutions responded that they may be required to make multiple adjustments within the same fiscal year. Even the best administrator cannot be expected to make prudent decisions when those same decisions may be immediately pre-empted. It is not difficult to understand why the following recommendations appeared frequently: "Develop short and long-range operating plans." "Be sure your long and short-term needs in facilities are known and well documented."

In fact, many would agree with the following advice:

> *Budgets should be developed on a 2, 3, 4, or 5-year basis, rather than just year-to-year as is now the case. This would allow for better planning and provide far more flexibility.*

Another member echoed similar thoughts:

> *Be proactive—that is, be involved in decisions and search for new operating strategies which protect the long-term objectives of the facilities department.*

Strategic planning has becoming more popular and perhaps better defined in recent years. It is reassuring to know that facilities managers are now gaining more insight into the strategic planning process and becoming more comfortable when asked to participate. Most would, however, caution that it is a rather intense project.

The survey comments also revealed feelings that some college and university presidents use the campus (or facilities) funds to promote their own agendas, for example:

> *Short-term presidents who plan to beat the problem by leaving town are our bane. We need leaders [who] know they must solve the problem today to avoid bigger problems tomorrow.*

Another respondent provided an example of this type of problem. The president sought to use the endowment principal as a means of avoiding the inevitable reduction of expenditures, but failed; in the meantime, the campus suffered severe deterioration of the building structures.

Perhaps the most distressing comments were those from facilities managers who were deeply concerned about the manner in which decisions were being made.

The university is using short-term management techniques (personnel reductions) to solve long-term institutional problems.

Budget constraints are not new by any means and, as indicated at the start of this chapter, it is difficult to envision a facilities administrator who has not faced some sort of budget problem; most have seen the problem get worse over the years. The truth is, reduced staff must be accomplished by reduced service expectations—one cannot "do more with less" forever.

There were additional suggestions regarding what the level of service should be during financially constrained times. To start, however, the following seems to be universally agreed upon: be an active participant in the process, making sure to document what resources are required to provide levels of service. Also, tie reductions in services with reduction in budget and communicate this information well.

Communication

The importance of communication was emphasized by respondents throughout the survey. Respondents offered the following suggestions:

Do not become defensive. Provide a clear statement of the impact of the proposed reduction.

Clearly define the scope of reductions and their potential impact.

Remember to clearly state the "loss in service" which will result from cuts, publicize and have [the] president, vice president "buy into it."

Develop guidelines to prioritize your service responsibilities and communicate these to the campus community, as well as the physical plant staff.

Provide the best environment possible with the dollars available.

Garnering support for change has been alluded to throughout this chapter. In Table 4, we have summarized the groups whom our respondents felt supported their efforts at their institutions.

Several facilities departments were given the opportunity to demonstrate what services they felt should be cut or at least

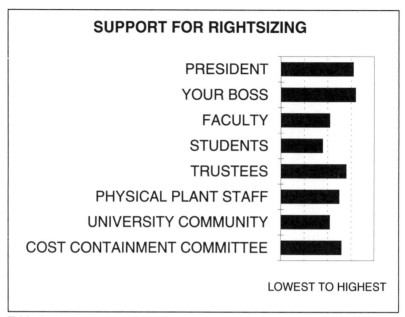

SUPPORT FOR RIGHTSIZING

PRESIDENT
YOUR BOSS
FACULTY
STUDENTS
TRUSTEES
PHYSICAL PLANT STAFF
UNIVERSITY COMMUNITY
COST CONTAINMENT COMMITTEE

LOWEST TO HIGHEST

Table 4.
Level of support for rightsizing efforts by group.

reduced, given the mandated (reduced) budget guidelines. Some were asked to identify several scenarios, depending on the eventual size of the institutional budget cut.

Perhaps the preferred process should be one in which the facilities administrator presents to the budget committee options from which to choose, each stating the number of positions that would have to be cut and the services that would be eliminated. Some respondents indicated that they had sought the advice of a "facilities committee" composed of customers who represented a fair cross-section of the community.

Interestingly, the most enlightening aspect of discussions within such a committee can be how it highlights differences in department size and the availability of "soft" money (e.g., funds from grants and other research). These variations often set the large research schools apart from the smaller, often liberal arts faculty, whose departments usually have very little "discretionary" funds.

This scenario can be taken one step further if the institution will agree to special conditions, such as permitting academic department to pay the facilities department for services beyond the norm. Similarly, departments may wish to adjust (or buy) service schedules to fit their particular needs, as long as the total number of staff needed remains constant. One respondent from a large university with a medical center (and therefore more "soft" money) did cost out all services and permitted the customers to pick exactly which services they wanted to pay for. The customer could, for example, increase custodial service in public areas while reducing the painting schedule. While this may satisfy the customers, however, it can result in additional paperwork and confusion as workers are moved around.

One respondent cautioned, however, that "creativity frequently culminates in short-term efficiency and long-range demise." Perhaps a good compromise is "Move logically; do the best you can and don't worry."

More than anything else, the survey revealed a deep concern for the consequences of reducing facilities funding. The most obvious, at least to facilities administrators, is the general degradation in the quality of services. As mentioned earlier, in happier times past, facilities departments could provide almost anything the campus community desired. Facilities officers just asked for additional resources, using the demand for new and improved services as justification. Although the early retirement programs have thinned the ranks of the faculty who grew accustomed to the amenities and considered them sacred, such niceties as custodial staff break areas (and even staff coffee cups) may still be considered "necessary" by some members of the community.

At my former institution, most of the high-rise buildings had fixed sashes. The exterior sides could only be washed by a contractor using OSHA-approved equipment. When the school administrators decided to stop washing these exterior windows due to the high cost of that contracted service, the quality of life truly suffered. (These same administrators had windows that could be washed by the cleaning staff!) Looking at the world through glass colored by years of grime affects the tenant's outlook on life in general. Other services, perhaps less obvious to the typical customer, also suffered. Respondents noted that "The reduction of manpower has resulted in a less attractive campus that impacts all users."

Referring again to the strategic plan, one member summed it up.

> *[Aim for] graceful degradation [by setting] priorities. [Use] a strategic facilities plan that prioritizes how [the] level of services will be reduced.*

No one reading this chapter will be surprised to learn that respondents identified the problem of long-term deferred maintenance more often than any other concern, and for that reason, I will not dwell on that issue, except to quote some of the more eloquent responses.

> *The effects of deferred maintenance are not felt by the management generation that defers the maintenance to balance the budget. As facilities age, maintenance needs increase exponentially. Together these two conditions portend facility disaster.*

Another, paraphrasing the above.

> *Deferred maintenance increases, causing infrastructure decay, which will amount to large capital investments to correct. As personnel are cut, services are also cut, thus becoming a vicious circle of failure.*

Concluding as we began, it is not difficult to understand why we are where we are, but I am hopeful that advice from our colleagues may provide some insights that will enable us to better cope with the difficulties of these times. At the very least, as the saying goes, "misery loves company," and knowing that you are not alone in this fight to maintain the integrity of your facilities in spite of past (and perhaps future) budget cuts may be reassuring. If not, then few can disagree with the most thought provoking comment of all: "Find a growing university and go there!"

Notes

1. A recent example of such a cut occurred in early February 1995 at the State University of New York. The thirty-two SUNY campuses developed preliminary 1994-95 budgets in late 1993, and revised them through early 1994 as state projections changed. In April 1994 the budget was finally approved and appropriations for each campus established. On February 1, 1995, however—nearly ten months after the fiscal year began—newly elected Governor George Pataki announced that SUNY must cut expenditures by $25 million. Furthermore, that $10 million must be cut by March 31, 1995, despite the fact that classes had been in session since January.

Appendix

Case Study 1

When it comes to rightsizing, one facilities manager at a large midwestern university has seen it all. Bill first experienced the process nearly twenty years ago, and has had similar experiences at three separate institutions, ranging in size from a small college to a major public institution. As one might anticipate, the process always begins in the same way; only the results differ. Perhaps that's why Bill advises others to "set priorities before the crisis and do not yield to politics. You will need a lot of communication to help the campus understand the situation."

Bill first experienced rightsizing as an observer; a mid-level supervisor in a larger institution in the mid seventies when institutions were growing more rapidly than their budgets. Because that public institution was constrained from converting non-salary dollars into staff, the easy answer was to defer staffing increases as the campus grew. Frankly, this process may have more merit than attrition, because the reductions are spread across the board, whereas attrition results in arbitrary reduction and can affect one area much more drastically than another.

Bill's next experience was at a small college that received no state support. Fearful that attrition might eliminate some key position (e.g., the only locksmith) or that someone would suggest that they forego preventive maintenance, Bill was aware that some pre-planning was clearly necessary. He and his senior staff elected to involve their employees, hoping that by building ownership, they could avert disaster. Unit heads met with employees, soliciting suggestions regarding cross-training. They discussed those tasks that they felt were unnecessary or ineffective. He cautions however, that one must be prepared to deal appropriately with the recommendation to cut the number of supervisors! Bill was confident that the effort to involve all of the staff placed them in the best position to weather the storm.

At his current institution, the decision to rightsize was prolonged to the point where the board of directors became involved and immediate significant reductions were necessary. The vice presidents delivered their "hit lists" and the entire institution was in shock! Fortunately, his previous experiences had caused Bill to recognize the early warnings, and he had already begun to trim his staff by attrition and cross-train the rest. Services were cut and priorities amended, all in a controlled fashion. As might be expected, the rumor mill was running at full speed, and facilities personnel were in the middle of these conversations on a daily basis. Naturally, they were concerned about their own future.

To combat rumors, Bill and his supervisory staff again initiated a "communications" phase. They spent a lot of time at the lunch tables and in the shops. Supervisors told their staff to avoid gossip and to make sure that they were as productive as possible, recognizing that perceptions are very important when everyone is concerned. He concluded our discussion with the advice that it is best to be up front with staff. Morale clearly improved within his units, especially when they recognized that their department had avoided the dire consequences that had affected others.

Case Study 2

Facilities need not be the only area cut, nor the hardest hit, although that is the common feeling among facilities administrators. Jon, the vice president for administration at a mid-Atlantic state community college advises administrators to "recognize reality early, be honest, open, and fair, but do what is necessary." When questioned in more detail, he indicated that his institution, like many others, went through a period of denial. Not only did they experience a 10 percent cut in their budget, but it hit in the middle of a fiscal year, near the end of summer after some faculty had been hired for the fall semester. However, Jon's division had recognized reality earlier than some, and had taken the opportunity, when presented, to "cut some of the dead wood." Even so, when the reduction was put into force, some facilities personnel had to be terminated. But at least the department was in a better position to respond.

Jon cautions that there is an overriding need to make sure that the institution remains viable during and after the rightsizing process. We are well aware that educational institutions are labor intensive and, therefore, staff reductions are inevitable. As has become the norm, Jon's institution did attempt to accomplish those reductions through a combination of attrition and a freeze on hiring any replacements pending specific justification. Further, the justification process was not typical. In order to fill a vacant position, all of the vice presidents had to agree on the need. As a result, only a few positions were filled, although some adjunct faculty were hired. From an institutional perspective, the vice presidents were "forced" to become more aware of the operations of all sectors of the college. Jon believes this worked to the benefit of his facilities operations, inasmuch as the vice presidents, in effect, represented the customers and, as such, were more open to customers' needs for services.

Perhaps Jon's most startling revelation was a cost-reduction measure offered by the support staff, in particular, the facilities group. Everyone agreed to a reduction in salary and leave credits (vacation/sick time)! They were willing to sacrifice their individual benefits in order to preserve the institution.

The college president convened meetings each week to review the status of the state funding. At these meetings, everyone could ask questions and offer suggestions. Many suggestions (like the salary reductions referred to earlier) that at first were thought to be minor, later became quite significant. For example, every publication received was reviewed for need. The mailing lists for all publications were also reviewed, and it was discovered that some persons were receiving multiple copies.

Efficiency improvements were recommended, and the facilities department was permitted to purchase equipment items that would reduce labor. Jon did admit that the cuts in facilities units were, in some cases, too severe. In order to justify recovering some positions, the college did its own benchmarking, focusing on other institutions in the "system." Those surveys confirmed that certain areas were overstaffed, while others needed to be strengthened. This situation may have been the result of attrition patterns which, unfortunately, do not necessarily reflect institutional needs. However, the data from the benchmarking study were sufficient to support additional personnel in those understaffed areas.

Perhaps the most significant benefit in the downsizing process was the net sense of trust that formed within that institution. Even after the crisis, the president continued his forums and the vice presidents developed a better understanding of the entire college operation. As Jon states, the institution should come through the rightsizing process with health and wholeness.

Case Study 3

Few will question that the need to reduce budgets while maintaining services has led to many creative responses. And, while what works for one institution may not work for another, all avenues must be explored, even those which initially seem impossible. Robert, facilities manager at a university health center in the eastern United States, recommended "manage organizational structure to reduce the size of the organization and reduce overhead costs." This advice might at first sound rather elementary and commonplace; however, when Robert was interviewed to explore those thoughts in more detail, it became clear that his experiences were not so common.

Robert's institution used the following process to restructure its management structure. Following each vacancy at the professional level, the former position description was examined. Not *only was the specific need for the position considered before a vacant position was filled, but the salary level and the position's relationship to other, similar positions was reviewed. Duties were examined to determine if they could be divided up and assigned to others. If no other options were possible, the vacancy was filled as originally defined. The health center found, however, that because of the shaky economy in the state, they could attract extremely well qualified persons, sometimes at a lower starting salary. As a result, not only have they reduced their overhead costs (between 25 and 50 percent in some cases), but, with as many as 170 applications for one position, they have also attracted some exceptional talent.*

As a public institution, the health center is a unionized shop whose employees are entitled to benefits typical of those negotiated by a public employee union contract. Wages have become quite generous and clearly well above the minimum typical of other service industries. Further, public employees enjoy liberal leave benefits such as vacation, sick, and personal time off. In fact, even when fully staffed, on average, nearly 15 percent of employees were off at any one time. The union contracts further stated that no employee could lose his or her job to outside contractors.

While this environment seems to offer little opportunity for change, the health center was able to use attrition to reduce staff and position itself for change. Little by little, as areas were restructured, particularly those with more narrowly defined responsibilities, the health center has begun to contract for custodial services. The hourly rates for contractors in this case are considerably less than the public employee rates of pay and the contractor is obligated to maintain staffing at 100 percent for each shift, regardless.

The center has retained the original supervisory positions, converting some into contract managers. According to Robert, these managers seem to react more positively to customer complaints, now that they need only to pick up a phone and pass that complaint on to the contractor. Overall, Robert estimates a savings of 40 percent in labor costs while maintaining 100 percent coverage.

Robert attributes the health center's successful restructuring efforts to the organization's ability to change with the times and to quality of personnel available in today's marketplace.

Case Study 4

At the two Stonybrook campuses of the State University of New York, the facilities departments jointly developed what they referred to as a Service Inventory. That document, over 100 pages long, details the services provided by all the departments, which report to the assistant vice president for facilities operations. Each activity (custodial, painting, etc.) is shown at the current level and the costs of the tasks are published for zero service up to the current level. It also shows "future" enhanced services, including those services facilities operations would like to provide if in fact funding was available.

For example, carpet cleaning could be increased from the present schedule of spot cleaning to once or twice a year. If it is determined that the carpet cleaning is more important than certain other services, then levels of both must be altered; carpet cleaning up and the other service, down.

There are advantages and disadvantages to "offering" the administration, or worse, the customer, the opportunity to alter the service levels deemed most appropriate by the facilities professional. However, if one assumes that critical items such as preventive maintenance are "held harmless" and only items thought to be discretionary in nature are available for change, the system has great potential...and the facilities managers can no longer be blamed.

Rightsizing Through the Eyes of History

Pieter J. van der Have

From a historical perspective, the concept of rightsizing is nothing new. Known by many different names and applied under differing philosophies and circumstances, the need for it has existed as long as we have walked upright.

The ancient nomadic tribes frequently were forced to control the size of their economic units as soon as their immediate environments were no longer able to provide critical resources—or support their needs. The size of the tribe or clan was voluntarily and frequently involuntarily controlled through a number of processes: by nature (lack of food, for example), tribal warfare, or through community imposed means (leaving the old, the weak, and the sick behind), and in competition (battle).

Many millennia later the Romans conquered most of Europe and the Mediterranean territories. In only a relatively short period of time, they found it impossible to infinitely guarantee all resources required to manage or control what they conquered. At first their approach to rightsizing was to try to continue doing what they were doing (not redefining their objectives): they simply strived to enhance available manpower through the enlistment of increasingly older and younger men. Quickly, they discovered they were running out of virile men back home, limiting population growth. Then they enlisted the services of mercenaries, which provided only short-term success. Mercenaries, although tough soldiers, had no inclination to display the kind of patriotism and loyalty expected by the Roman commanders.

Mutiny was frequent. Morale, both at home and in the distant stretches, began to collapse. Where once there was pride, suddenly there was increased discontent and mutiny. The Roman legations more frequently found themselves under attack from those whom they were trying to control or from others who wanted what they had. They became unable to maintain their own standards, and eventually their resources were strained to where they had to pull back. Finally, a form of rightsizing was achieved when they were forced to retreat to within boundaries defined more by outsiders than by themselves.

We can look across history and find numerous reoccurrences of the same type of phenomenon. Charlemagne, Napoleon, Genghis Khan, Hitler, Richard Nixon—each one had an empire, yet at some time each one had to adjust his sights, his way of doing business—his strategic plans. These are examples of political rightsizing, but there are also historical illustrations in the business world. For example, the East India Company comes to mind. The large railroad companies of the more recent past are another. The movie industry was forced to take a close look at itself a number of times during the first half of this century. One common denominator is fairly evident in all of these historical illustrations of rightsizing: they were all economically necessitated.

The elements that comprise "economics" change from one period of history to the next. It remains indisputable that all historical examples of rightsizing are a product of that period's economic circumstances and the concurrent elements of competition. Few organizations have gone into rightsizing totally voluntarily. Invariably, external influences have caused them to rethink their strategies.

Rightsizing Across the World Today

It is evident that in more recent history not much has changed. In the early 1990s, Iraq's thwarted attempt to take over Kuwait was probably an effort to redefine its ability to sustain or improve its (right)size: Iraq needed access to the open seas. During the last two decades of the 20th century, the United States has been deeply involved with Japan and others in a highly nationalistic attempt at rightsizing. Within Japan, very large and generally very successful corporations have found themselves dealing with economic downturns through the use of rightsizing, or related variations. Sony and Toyota are certainly a couple of notable examples.

On shaky ground at the same time was the United States's import/export relationship with Europe. Each of the players in that relationship identified an almost religious mandate to position itself to respond to how it perceived its strategic plan and objectives. Within Europe, individual countries have had to deal with similar issues. In addition, many European companies have been rightsizing. Not too long ago, European automobile manufacturers laid off more than 60,000 employees. In Great Britain, Jaguar laid off nearly a thousand staff. In the Netherlands, Philips, the parent company of Norelco, showed staggering numbers of people the corporate door.

Rightsizing Within the United States

We are all woefully aware of headlines, past and present, that frighten the socks off every sensible working person in this country, from CEO to office clerk, from general to private, from president to window washer to middle manager.

Sears Cuts 6,900 Additional Jobs

AT&T to Cut its Payroll by 27,000

IBM to Cut Work Force by 14,000

Dupont to Cut 4,500 Chemical Employees

Our State to be Hit by Closure of Military Bases

General Motors Closes Five Plants

PG&E Jobs Go Down While Rates Go Up

United Technologies Cutting 11,000

UNISYS Lays Off 10,000

Eastern Airlines Lays Off Another 1,500 (and finally closes its corporate doors)

IBM To Reduce Staffing Levels By Another 20,000

Clearly, each of these business entities was seeking to find the right size. The guiding light for these adjustments is often the corporate perception of its ideal but trimmed size, considering available resources and the marketplace (economics, share of the market, piece of the pie). Unfortunately, many corporate executives have traditionally misunderstood the significance of corporate rightsizing. Roger Smith, CEO of General Motors during the 1980s, was once asked to explain the situation GM found itself in. His answer—"I don't know. It is a mysterious thing."—was not reassuring, but was typical of the dilemma in which American business often found and likely still finds itself.

What Is Rightsizing?

American executives have long suffered from a misperception. Rightsizing has never been a way of cutting short-term costs by simply reducing the size of the front line or the scope of services: it *is* making a long-term investment in restructuring the corporate systems to improve productivity and set the stage for strategically planned new growth.

The manner in which organizations achieve rightsizing may be highly unique. For example, in Japan some of the staff reductions were made possible by initiating a decentralized management system. In the United States until fairly recently, the push had been (more often than not) to layoff only front-line workers while, in some cases, insensitively continuing to pay senior officers disproportionate bonuses. Over the last thirty years, in various areas around the world, organizations have attempted to avert or avoid rightsizing by initiating hot-off-the-press new management techniques (Theory Z, BPR/BPT, MBO, TQM, Value Chain Analysis, Kaisen, and others). The result has been, according to the American Management Association, that only 45 percent of the companies that "rightsized" (benevolently used as a friendlier synonym for "downsized") showed any increase in profits in subsequent years. Many of them found they had to rightsize again in the next year, and the next, and the next.

For many organizations once widely recognized as leaders in their field (such as IBM and GM), rightsizing has become a common strategy to ensure survival in a recessionary economy. Too many of them did not recognize or were simply unaware that rightsizing must go hand in hand with innovation. Some of them were so hamstrung by their internal bureaucracies that implementing change was like pushing a rope uphill. For some, such as IBM, the success of rapid growth and success two decades before brought with it a bureaucracy solid as a rock. In 1970, the top echelon at General Motors developed a formula for success based purely on its giant success of prior years. The formula was totally naive, based on blatant misperceptions of the world marketplace and the consumer, and it damaged GM to the point where it still has barely recovered, and is yet showing some of the scars.

For similar reasons, many companies have had to rightsize more than once, perpetually striving to corral their elusive goals. These organizations were not really rightsizing. They were simply reducing staffing levels! Too often, rightsizing can better be described as "dumbsizing."

President Bill Clinton won votes through his campaign promise to create a leaner, more efficient government. The "National Performance Review" report presented by Vice President Al Gore in September 1993 was met with a substantial amount of enthusiasm by key individuals within and outside the government. After all, there were in 1994 over 2,155,000 full-time positions on the federal payrolls; 2,134,000 of which were filled. We taxpayers thought it would be great for the administration to reduce the size and the cost of this payroll. We felt only a slight pang of guilt when we heard this meant eliminating 118,000 jobs in the first two years, and another 134,000 within a few years after that. Reflecting the growing federal support for the "lean" and "total quality" schools of thought, the summary report recommended eliminating excessive regulations and bureaucratic layers over the next five years. Congress considered a federal "buy-out" program, whereby an agency could buy out qualifying participants' employment, perhaps for as much as $25,000!

Since strategic planning is a vital component of any rightsizing process (and this one no less so) time will be the judge of whether the federal brain trust has bought out the right employees, and eliminated the right bureaucracies.

Restructuring—Another Way of Saying Rightsizing?

There are a number of ways we managers distance ourselves from the emotional aspects of altering the organization. Rightsizing, when used primarily to improve ailing bottom lines, appears to be intended to reduce staff, thus merely serving as a form of downsizing, which sounds cold and calculating. "Rightsizing," on the other hand, has an almost religious or righteous sound to it. In our society, where we couch real feelings behind euphemisms, this is the term used most frequently. Some CEOs may find it easier to recite eloquent phrases when elaborating on the need and justifications for rightsizing.

Financial or corporate people may prefer to use the term "restructuring," which appears to presume a logical approach to dealing with whatever ails the organization. Over the last decade, Sears has announced a number of rightsizing efforts. For example, they have revised staffing levels, types of staff, product lines, etc. They later distanced themselves from and divested themselves of unprofitable ventures. They have closed many of their previously lucrative catalog outlets. In mid-1994, Sara Lee announced it was going to move into a rightsizing mode. Its announcement was more than just a small surprise, since the prior year had been the most successful ever. Sara Lee, wanting to avoid inefficiencies later on, decided to tackle this challenge before it was no longer an option. Its CEO decided to take this rare opportunity to look at the whole picture while the opportunity was there. Was this rightsizing or restructuring?

Simply stated, rightsizing, without holistically rethinking the strategic plan for the entire organization, may result in more than just reducing costs. Some of us may remember Studebaker or Eastern Airlines. Yet, naive is anyone who thinks strategic planning will solve all corporate shortcomings. We often assume that management can formulate a "master plan" that we can then follow religiously to get us to where we need to go. Corporate and organizational leaders must realize that equally important to that journey is how an organization deals with miscalculation, mistakes, and generally unanticipated events. That is where the human element can make all the difference. Finally, one has to admit that plain luck will also have an impact. As managers or visioned leaders, we must set the stage for good luck to have the best chance to do the most good.

We suggest an answer to the haunting question: What is rightsizing? Although there are as many definitions of this term as there are of deferred maintenance, perhaps it can be reduced to this single paragraph.

RIGHTSIZING is a systematic approach to analyzing an organization's total hierarchy, systems, organizational structures and priorities, staffing levels and qualifications, information and product flows. This is accomplished by adding, deleting, and changing elements as necessary to ensure that every component of the organizational environment contributes completely and only to the organization's mission and strategic plan, while recognizing that the human aspect is the most critical component of the process.

Several elements can be examined closely in pursuing the rightsizing process:

- Human resources/liabilities (staffing, management issues)
- Standards of service (quality, quantity)
- Customers served
- Capital/physical resources and liabilities

As the private sector in the United States continues trimming its workforce, the reverberations of those reductions will unavoidably be felt by those in other sectors who rely on funds generated by the private sector as their life blood. A positive aspect to all of this is that there may be a greater number of well-qualified applicants in the labor pool looking for work, and they may be willing to work for less. On the flipside, there are also more under-qualified applicants. Effective screening methods thus become more critical. And, more management consultants find more work.

Rightsizing in Higher Education

God, grant me the serenity to accept the things I cannot change,
courage to change those things I can, and wisdom to know the
difference.

—Serenity Prayer

Historically Speaking

Rightsizing in the private sector understandably affects dona-
tions, grants, tax revenues, student enrollments, ability to pay
rising tuition costs, and so forth. This must then be taken in
tandem with the decreasing level of respect higher education
is receiving from its general constituency. Higher education is
liberally accused of being elitist, having inefficient administrative bureaucracies, providing poor teachers, offering anachro-
nistic programs through incoherent curricula—all that at
unaffordable prices. Higher education faces at least as great a
challenge as does any corporation in the private sector. It's
different, yet it's the same!

Kit Lively, in *The Chronicle of Higher Education* (Feb. 3, 1993),
indicated that state universities and colleges are rightsizing
their curricula to meet budget cuts imposed by cash-strapped
state governments. Often the criteria for the programs try to
involve numerical determinants such as low enrollments or low
graduation rates. Some institutions, such as Pennsylvania
State University, have reviewed the success of their academic
programs, and have chosen to modify or eliminate a number
of them. Other administrations, such as the one at Syracuse
University, have undertaken a significant step toward rightsizing through implementation of a campus-wide TQM program.
All of this suggests a rational, logical, systematic, and informed
process.

NACUBO (National Association of College and University
Business Officers) revealed in a recent publication that thirty
states had made mid-year higher education cuts averaging 3.9
percent in 1990-91. Twenty-one states expected reductions in
the following year as well. The remainder anticipated budget
increases below inflation. In APPA's more recent rightsizing
survey, over 50 percent of the respondents indicated they had
experienced budget reductions of more than 3 percent in the
last five years. A number of institutions have seen the percentage of the budget pie normally allocated to facilities dwindling

from double percentage figures to single digits. There is every indication this trend is likely to continue into the next century. Undoubtedly, it will start affecting institutions previously left relatively unscathed.

In NACUBO's *Business Officer* (March 1994), Terrence E. Deal and William A. Jenkins offer this opinion:

> *Managers, including higher education administrators, are often pre-occupied with quick-fix solutions, short-term results, and a belief that rational analysis and rightsizing solve any problem. This mindset leads many well-intentioned people to sterilize the human side of organizations. They believe that strategy, decisions, and structure are all that matter.*

Level of Involvement by Facilities Professionals

Of significance among the responses offered by APPA members through the aforementioned survey was their perception of their level of involvement in the decision-making processes. A majority indicated the key decisions regarding trimming the budget were made at higher levels, above that of the chief facilities professional. A majority also felt they received less support than they should have from their administrations regarding reasonable implementation of new or adjusted programs. Comments indicated respondents felt their input was either not solicited or considered. (Survey comments are discussed in detail in the chapter, Results of the Rightsizing Survey.

A reasonable conclusion is that there is room and, in fact, a mandate for improved planning processes in higher education, just like there is in the private sector. Not too surprisingly, many facilities professionals felt they have in the past not been given many or any options. Across-the-board cuts have been the rule rather than the exception. Some fear their senior administrators have not grasped the impact of inferior facilities programming and maintenance. This possibly unfair or incorrect perception among senior administrators can affect whether facilities officers are able to rightsize successfully when (not if) the need arises.

Virtually all of the comments APPA received in response to its survey suggested that each institution needs to look at its situation holistically when shifting into a rightsizing phase. Rightsizing the facilities management areas, according to these professionals, always has to be accompanied by a similar effort on the academic side, with open and honest communication between the two. Comments indicate a strong preference on the part of higher education facilities professionals to proceed with a team approach to developing the institution's plan. They not only prefer that, they feel it is highly essential toward successful rightsizing.

On page 35, elements of rightsizing were identified in a general sense. Revisiting them with a higher education bias produces these elements:

- Human resources (staffing and management opportunities)
- Standards of service (quality and quantity)
- Customers/departments/facilities served (potential reallocation of costs)
- Space utilization (more effective use of space)

Elements of Rightsizing

Rightsizing Using the Standards Programs

A naval shipyard in Charleston, South Carolina, combined activity-based costing and value-added analysis techniques to make support activities transparent and intelligible. They restructured support functions and selected necessary activities to improve cost and performance. Activity-based costing was found to be an ideal foundation for rightsizing. Standards programs provide a solid foundation toward proceeding with an activity-based costing analysis.

Front-line staff can help evaluate standards and programs. The effective leader knows and listens to the front line through MBBT (Management By Being There), frequently learning from the folks who really know how things work. The people on the front line are often eager to share information on programs which are effective, programs which are not providing desired results, or possible some which need to be added, modified, or deleted. Through involvement of representatives from the entire campus community, both from within and outside the facilities organization, each can learn from and educate the others.

Implementation and Looking Back

Downsizing within the facilities area was not optional at the University of Utah years ago. In 1987, the institution's administration determined it was time to show the state legislature that the University of Utah was not going to allow its components to get fat. Thus, all departments were required to review their individual budgets and programs for the purpose of realigning institutional budgets. A committee made up mostly of representatives from the non-support side was established to evaluate the data and make recommendations. Fortunately, the facilities organization had established a number of excellent standards programs many years earlier—in some cases decades earlier. Reasonable criteria for making informed decisions were readily available.

Members of the committee reviewed the options and reached consensus on which standards could best be altered or eliminated with only minimal negative impact on academic programs. (In our opinion, the investment in the campus's physical investments and the infrastructure was not given equal consideration.) Some good things resulted of this process as well. The campus had forever emptied each and every waste basket every day. The program has been restructured to accommodate individual needs of the various types of areas, rather than treating them all the same. Thus, office waste baskets are emptied only once a week.

Interior paint schedules were stretched significantly. Certain grounds maintenance standards were modified, but not to the point where it would seriously or permanently detract from the general appearance of the campus.

A "shopping list" containing these and additional items was provided to this university's president. All campus organizations—academic, support, and auxiliary functions—went through the same exercise. The administration decided to have us eliminate close to 100 full-time positions in plant operations.

To the surprise of some, there were actually some benefits from this experience. For instance, the campus community discovered it had been living in an environment of luxury prior to the implementation of these reductions. Most offices do not need to be cleaned every day. In general, building occupants have noticed no alarming decrease in cleanliness. Most people are willing and able to adjust. Over a few years, through improved utilization of available resources, some reduced service levels have been reversed without increasing staff.

If staff and faculty at the University of Utah were to look back at this process, they might recognize an apparent absence of an institutional strategic plan. Thus, the departments' strategic plans (for those who had one) were based on thin air. For most of the departments responding to the call for budget realignment, the question asked was "What can we cut out that is the least worthwhile to this institution (today), and/or is not effective?"

The question that should have been asked, was: "What are we doing today that will (not) contribute to the institution's strategic plan over the next twenty to fifty years?"

Some processes or programs were eliminated which possibly should not have been. For example, we were told to stop washing windows. No one anticipated the impact this reduction would have on the attitude and the morale of the building occupants, and perhaps more significantly, the visitors. Similarly, certain academic programs were eliminated which were found to be highly essential just a few years later. Costs for certain services or functions were simply transferred from one cost center to another. These did not present a real cost savings, only the perception of one.

In facilities management we also found some services cannot be eliminated, especially those which concern public areas and laboratories. For example, waste baskets in biological research laboratories have to be emptied every day to prevent problems with odor and contamination. Uncarpeted hallways in high traffic buildings have to be cleaned on a daily basis when the snows fly, or the floor surfaces will be ground into oblivion. Substantially reducing filter changes on the air delivery systems proved impractical, because it can eventually affect energy efficiency and it increases the dirt and dust problem. We skirted reducing any program related to preventive maintenance of mechanical and electrical systems, for obvious reasons.

Other Rightsizing Options

In the traditional facilities or physical plant organization, there is a fairly well-defined management hierarchy. In many organizations, there is a director over one or more assistant directors, who manage supervisors, who are over leadworkers, who may lead senior technicians or journeymen, who then lead entry-level positions. Looking up, the director often sees first an associate or an assistant vice president (or assistant vice chancellor), then a vice president or a vice chancellor, perhaps then an executive vice president, or perhaps a provost, and then a president or chancellor who may answer to a system president. At the summit hovers a governing body.

A valid question is, can a tier of management be eliminated without affecting the operation and its success? Utility companies, traditionally loaded with tiers, have taken a look at themselves and have restructured using this approach. Organizations in the public sector, including agencies at federal and state levels, have flattened their traditional pyramids. This kind of effort can go a long way toward communicating the organization's sincerity in its rightsizing effort.

Rightsizing, if done effectively, looks at tiers of management in the pyramid. Often, outside influences may dictate the nature of the organization. However, opportunities exist to streamline an organization by reducing the number of individuals on any one tier. This can sometimes be accomplished by combining or eliminating operational responsibilities.

Steamlining can also be accomplished by refining support functions. Centralized operations may make a process more efficient. If planned carefully, an operation can be centralized by removing individuals from the remote organizational units and making them part of the central unit. Failure to include remote staff in the effort may result in additional staff in the centralized function and under-used employees in the outlying operations.

Rightsizing may also look at the way the work is being scheduled. Is shift work more appropriate (and less expensive) than is paying overtime? Could some tasks be performed by the private sector to reduce some of the overhead and benefits expenses? Many of us have shops fixed organizationally, based on trade specialties rigidly cast into the organization chart (such as a carpentry shop), each with its own supervisor. Perhaps it is more efffective to have result teams, where technicians and journeymen of various trades work together as a team for a common objective. For example, a team might accept total responsibility for maintaining and operating a precinct or sector of the campus, developing a sense of ownership for "their" buildings.

Improved utilization of current technology is often a way to control labor costs. Data from various surveys does not suggest an automatic inverse relationship between staffing levels and increased use of sophisticated technology. Frequently, staff efforts are simply redirected—which does not necessarily reduce costs, but may increase long-term effectiveness.

A simple question with a complicated answer may be: Are the campus's facilities being fully utilized? Can some be shut down or leased to other entities? Is it more cost-effective to tear down (being sensitive to historical values) old dinosaurs and, if needs be, build new, more efficient structures?

Conclusion

Higher education, and specifically facilities management, are now or will soon have to enter the world of rightsizing. We should not feel alone in this challenge. History has forced rightsizing upon all types of organizations, entities, political bodies, and individuals virtually since the advent of time. The challenge to leaders now is to grab the opportunity to rightsize before it becomes an absolute necessity. The challenge to facilities management leaders is to have the appropriate standards in place so that intelligent decisions can be made regarding the elimination or modification of ineffective programs. Strategic planning is an unavoidable must in the rightsizing process. This involves recognizing and considering all elements of the organization—both the physical and the human. Higher education has a number of options available to it to implement effective rightsizing programs. The economic community as well as all other stakeholders to higher education expect this process start now where it has not already done so, and to continue with it where it has.

A Change in Focus in a Time of Change

Scott Charmack

This year nearly 3 million jobs will be created in the United States. Yet the average American company is still shedding workers by the thousands. Companies throughout the economy are streamlining to become more competitive. No sector of the economy is immune. Higher education is also infected with this virus and the doctor has prescribed the cure—reduce costs. The process to reduce costs, often misrepresented as rightsizing, too often slashes costs without an understanding of the short and long term consequences. Many times this "quick draw" approach to cost reductions cuts not only costs but needed functions and services, ignoring the opportunity to obtain cost reductions through a more rational process. Unfortunately, we do not have a historical perspective to help guide our decisions in this relatively uncharted territory.

Throughout much of the nineteenth and twentieth centuries, American business set the performance standards for the rest of the world. During this period American companies served as organizational models. They changed the way we lived and provided us the highest standard of living. Unfortunately, these companies entered the last third of the twentieth century with the same basic business principles they perfected 100 years earlier.

Higher education is facing the same dilemma; we are approaching the twenty-first century with organizational models and perceptions developed in the nineteenth century. Until recently, the model appeared to work. Higher education in this country has been the envy of the world. Our institutions have provided the educated workforce that allowed American business to outperform its off-shore competitors. Higher education responded to the post-war boom to accommodate hundreds of thousands of new students. We developed new technologies and medical cures, educated the masses, and even survived government regulation. How higher education responds to the new challenges of constant change, competition, and dramatically restricted resources will affect our ability to succeed, and possibly even to survive.

The crisis that we face today is not simply the result of budget cuts and reduced enrollment. It stems primarily from our industry's failure to adapt to a changing environment. We have not become attuned to a changing environment, nor have we adopted managerial and organizational styles to better predict and respond to customer requirements, technological changes, and our competition. Most of us have not even acknowledged that we have competition. To survive we must become customer-focused, manage with the goal of predicting and adapting to change, and stay ahead of our competition.

As facilities managers, we cannot directly influence course offerings, instructional delivery systems, or admissions standards, implement new instructional technology, or in any other way modify the academic function of the university. However, our institutions cannot succeed in accomplishing their mission without us. Then why is it that physical plant budgets are usually the first to be reduced? One probable reason is that we do not always understand what the institution really wants and needs us to do. We really do not understand or focus on our customers' needs, adapt to a changing environment, or check our competition.

Over the past twenty years the field of facilities management has become much more sophisticated. One measure of this is the evolution of the subject matter and focus of APPA's annual meeting. The focus has changed dramatically, as has the sophistication of the individuals entering the profession. The focus of these meetings has paralleled our own initiatives as facilities managers and might resemble the following progression:

Technological—The importance of a properly tuned boiler or the energy efficiency of Plant A to Plant B.

Accountability—What our management expects of us and how we demonstrate our stewardship of the resources for which we are responsible.

Professionalism—Increased emphasis on modern management and leadership.

Marketing—How to sell our program to the campus and gather support for our services.

Customer Service—The need to keep our customers satisfied with the services that we offer.

Quality Service—The need to improve the quality of services through such techniques as total quality management, business process reengineering, etc.

This evolution has incrementally changed how we do business. We have been progressively improving our organizations. Unfortunately, the world has been changing faster than our organizations. This can be likened to pole vaulting, where the bar just keeps getting higher. What was high enough last year may not qualify you this year. The result is that few institutions have kept the pace with our changing environment and are struggling to get over the bar without knocking it down. The dramatic budget reductions that many institutions have faced over the past decade have only exacerbated the situation.

Rightsizing is not simple cost cutting. Downsizing, budget containment, freezes, and so forth, are processes to cut costs. Rightsizing is an organized, carefully planned program to focus on institutional mission and customer requirements, manage costs, adapt to change, and remain competitive. It is, or should be, a highly focused process to reduce and control costs without sacrificing primary institutional goals.

Rightsizing is like a freight train barreling down the track. You cannot stop it by standing in front of it; you probably will not even slow it down. Your choices are few. You can jump on board or view the underside of the rightsizing train as it rolls over you. Theory would suggest that rightsizing should

1. Include the entire institution (academic and support operations).
2. Be based on the institution's mission and strategic plan.
3. Be implemented over time to ensure thorough planning and minimize impact (layoff, graduation, etc.).

Real world conditions (yes, higher education must now take its rightful place in the real world) would suggest that this theoretical model requires some adjusting because:

1. Our institutions traditionally change very slowly and are highly political, and rightsizing requires questioning fundamental institutional assumptions.
2. Campuses may have outdated mission statements and strategic plans—if they have any at all.
3. Financial constraints may not provide time for thorough planning and implementation.

Given these constraints, some might conclude that rightsizing is not feasible. Our experience is to the contrary; rightsizing is the *only* realistic means for us to become competitive. And while it is most effective when implemented campus-wide, it is still viable on a divisional or even a departmental basis.

The CSU Long Beach Experience

At California State University at Long Beach, the maintenance budget for the campus has been consistently reduced over the past fifteen years, yet the voters generously supported capital projects through bond financing that dramatically increased the size of the campus. Today, the physical plant budget is approximately the same size as it was more than twenty years ago when the campus was just half its current size. Other workload indicators have also had dramatic impacts on resource requirements. These include

- Aging facilities
- Increased utilization of facilities (longer hours of operation, increased use by outside groups, increased need to generate revenue from facilities, etc.)

- New building codes
- New health and safety codes
- New demands from changing instructional and research technology
- Ever increasing legislatively mandated programs and requirements

An ever increasing workload, constantly decreasing resources, and a managerial and organizational philosophy based on our historical perspective had resulted in a decline of the campus's physical environment. Our reaction to more work and fewer resources was to work harder and reduce services. We attempted to get the campus to lower their service expectations, and for a time this worked. However, even as our resources continued to be reduced and new buildings opened, the expectations and frustrations of the campus community grew.

The path to our current perspective was one of evolution. We reacted to reduced resources with the historical perspective that had guided our previously decisions. Looking back, we can clearly see how we got to our current state. In fact, our reactions can be grouped into three distinct phases of the evolution of our current management philosophy.

The first phase was characterized by an effort to improve efficiency, reduce nonproductive time, and seek a means to get more work from fewer employees using traditional techniques. Consultants were hired to examine various aspects of our operation. Emphasis was placed on purchasing materials and equipment that were intended to improve efficiency. To improve the tracking of work, labor, and materials, a computerized maintenance management system was purchased. The campus also experimented with alternative work shifts. However, reductions were taken in vacant positions and by cutting temporary staff and operating expenses. These reductions were accomplished without layoffs, though services were reduced and/or heavily backlogged. The emphasis was on avoiding layoffs, not necessarily on minimizing service problems.

The second phase of the reductions caused considerable frustration among all staff. It was at this point that the rest of the campus started to see their own budgets constrained. The physical plant budget had already been reduced approximately

15 to 20 percent and, based on our traditional approach, it seemed that our only means to deal with the magnitude of forthcoming budget cuts was through service reductions.

While we continued to seek improvements in our operational efficiency, these improvements could not keep pace with the budget reductions we were facing annually. These service reductions took the form of restricting availability, reducing frequencies, or eliminating services altogether. In some cases services were still offered, but on a recharge basis. While input was solicited from the campus prior to each reduction, the impact was not appreciated. We had hoped that through consultation the expectations of the campus might be modified to reflect our limited resources. As time went on, the reverse happened. As the cuts increased, the impact was more pronounced, and campus frustration increased and was focused on physical plant. Years of frustration over little things were magnified with their current impatience. Layoffs also began during this phase, and our employees began to question their job security and the institution's long-term commitment to protecting its investment in our facilities.

In the meantime, the state's financial outlook was bleak and not expected to improve for a number of years. We knew that our future included additional reductions. Our choice was either to continue to pursue traditional means to improve efficiency and continue to reduce services, or to fundamentally change our approach. The choice was simple—something radical had to happen. If we continued to reduce services, the campus at some point would ask whether our department was needed at all.

Our decision for radical change was based not so much on reduced resources but on the answers to these seemingly innocuous questions.

1. Is there anything that we do that could not be done by someone else in another department or by an outside company?

2. How would the faculty, staff, students, alumni, and supporters of our institution answer the first question?

3. How would our competitors answer the first question?

4. What is our real mission/purpose, and do our employees understand what our mission is?

5. Who are we providing services for?

Our search for answers to these questions has generated some response, while at the same time posing many new questions.

A Framework for Change

The answers to these questions and the new, unanswered questions only heightened our resolve to make fundamental changes in our operation. Something had to give. We did not have the means to increase our budget; therefore, we had to change somehow the way we provided services and the perception of the campus community. We talked to numerous campuses and organizations engaged in various forms of TQM, reengineering, etc. We interviewed more than a dozen consulting firms, and of course, we scanned the literature. This search turned up the following alternatives.

- Hire additional consultants to find means to further increase efficiency
- Implement some form of TQM.
- Implement Business Process Reengineering (BPR).
- Hire a public relations firm to convince the campus that we were really the good guys and that the reduced service levels that we were offering were really good for them.
- Contract out services.
- Some combination of the above.

After a good deal of thought, we chose TQM with the understanding that we would implement BPR and other alternatives once we had established the TQM framework. The aim of this chapter, however, is not to sell you on TQM. Rather, it is to provide some alternatives to business as usual with fewer resources. The change is philosophical but it can make a great difference in your approach to providing services. This philosophical difference can be implemented through a variety of methods. The vehicle for change will vary for each campus based upon managerial styles, the campus environment, and so forth. Therefore, we are not promoting TQM, BPR, or any other managerial method. We are, however, promoting a managerial evolution that includes the following concepts:

1. Define your mission around customer service.
2. Know your environment and plan for change.
3. Think of your department as a business enterprise.
4. Incorporate quality into your culture.
5. Strive for constant improvement.
6. Empower your employees.

Vision and Mission

The beginning of our journey began with the realization that we needed to change. The second step was to create a vision of what we wanted to be. This vision would then become the criterion against which we would measure our progress. As in any journey, we needed to visualize where we were going before we could begin to chart our course.

With the help of a facilitator, our plant operations department created a steering team and set out to assess where we were and develop a vision of what we wanted to be. This included scrapping our existing mission statement and developing a strategic plan.

The department had developed a mission statement years ago. We wrote it, paraded it around, and shoved in a drawer to gather dust. It reflected what our organization thought we were supposed to do. It basically stated that *we maintained and modified facilities.* We assumed that our employees and the rest of the campus concurred with our mission. The simple fact is that our "customers" had a much different concept of what our mission was. Not too surprisingly, it was more inclusive than our own concept. And our employees had their own concept as well.

Remember, our prior mission stated that we maintained facilities. It did not even recognize that we had "customers." When was the last time a building called you to complain? We basically determined what services would be provided, how often, and by whom. On the other hand, our current mission statement states that *we provide our customers facility related services.* This is not simply a word game to satisfy our TQM consultant. To us it was a fundamental change in our approach to providing service. More on this later.

Prior to rewriting our mission statement, we believed that we were customer oriented. We consulted and made adjustments to meet customer needs. We provided options for access to our services. We talked about customer service. We believed that our mission was to maintain facilities. When we changed our mission to customer-focused services we were forced to view our role differently, much differently. That meant first of all, we needed to spend more time understanding what our customers wanted, when they wanted it, and, of course, how to lower the cost of providing the requested service. For us this really meant that we had to examine what we did and how we did it, and if we did it at all. This is not an easy transition for any department.

We also understood that we had building occupants. They were the ones who were kind enough to call us and complain about one thing or another. We might have even called them customers. In hindsight, however, we did not treat them like customers. At least, not how we would have expected to be treated by the companies from which we bought services. In many ways we responded to our customers like the monopoly we were—take it our way or do without.

Other the past five years we have made efforts to improve our customer service. We provided training on how to greet the public, how to handle "problem" customers (that's an interesting concept), etc. But this is the Hollywood facade to customer service; merely window dressing. It did not change the underlying vision of what we were. When we changed our mission statement, it also meant that we needed to change our emphasis, approach, and assumptions on what we did and how we did it.

When plant operations adopted a customer-oriented philosophy, we needed to understand what our customers wanted and needed for facilities related services. We also needed to understand the changing nature of consumerism in this country. Americans have been very indifferent consumers. We have put up with mediocre service for generations. Our expectations for poor service became a self-fulfilling prophecy. As a result, good service was the exception, not the rule. However, this is rapidly changing. As more companies begin quality programs, their service improves and the consumers of their products and services, as well as their own employees, become more demanding consumers. They are, therefore, less likely to accept poor quality service. As more companies respond to competition with quality programs, the standard continues to rise for the entire service and manufacturing industry.

The same is true in higher education. Our customers are consumers of our services and also consumers of services from outside firms, both within and outside the university. Their expectations are constantly being elevated and we must find the means to meet these expectations.

This was certainly the case at our institution. As we became more aware of our own deficiencies in the eyes of our customers, we became more convinced of the need to change our focus. This has resulted in a new vision and mission for our department.

In theory your mission statement must complement the university's mission statement. However, if your institution has not updated their mission statement, adopt a mission statement that focuses on where you think the institution is headed, and head that way now. It's not perfect, but it's better than sitting around waiting. In that way you can use the time to begin to make substantial changes while the university updates its mission.

Change

As an industry, higher education has been slow to adapt to the changing environment. This is in part due to our internal focus, the political impact of adapting to changing conditions, and our reliance on traditional, time-tested organizational and managerial models. We've already discussed that our customers and our competitors have changed. Today we are seeing that the pace of change is accelerating and is pervasive in our society; therefore, it has never been more important to understand this changing environment in which we must compete. We must learn to predict the direction of change and, most importantly, adapt to these changes.

On the academic side of the house, we need to predict where student demand, jobs, research opportunities, etc., will be. We must anticipate what technology will be needed in the classrooms and laboratories, and how information will be utilized, transferred, transmitted, transformed, and stored. On the facilities side of the house, we need to predict the direction of these elements and also where our competitors are going, what technology will be available and how we might utilize it, what impact government regulations may have and how to mitigate or capitalize on them, and, most importantly, what our customers will need from us to be successful in their goals.

Like death and taxes, change is certain. What is also certain is if we want to survive we must incorporate the notion of constant change into our culture. We must choose change, not chase it or fight it.

Manage Your Department as a Business Enterprise

Over the years, physical plant has spent a good deal of time and resources trying to become more efficient. "Efficiency" was measured in relative terms to our past performance or to the performance of other universities. Since we really had not considered ourselves a business enterprise, we did not spend much time observing how our competitors did business. We were different. So different that comparison (benchmarking) did not make sense.

Remember that we stated earlier that our earlier performance was based primarily on models nearly 100 years old. It was also based on the notion that we did not have to compete with anyone for the services that we have traditionally provided. Without that competitive environment we've become complacent. We were not constantly pushing for improvements to stay ahead of our competitors because we simply did not recognize them as competitors.

Like many campuses, we had talked about how businesses ran their enterprises and wished that we were allowed to run our operations in a similar manner. Somehow we always concluded that the campus, system, state, board, etc., had too many rules and procedures to allow us to compete. So we simply tried to improve our existing operation within our existing internal and external bureaucracy. As a result, we fell further behind our outside competitors. But these folks were

not content with their present business. They had the brass
to go after our jobs.

If we are serious about competing, we must adopt the best
practices of our competitors. We must seek way to continuously improve our operation, service quality, and costs. We
acted like the U.S. auto industry. At one time, they controlled
the market share of domestically purchased automobiles to
such an extent that they hardly noticed when the Japanese
starting importing vehicles into this country. Over the span of
two decades these imports went from almost no market share
to more than one-third of all new vehicles sold in the United
States.

Facilities managers are in the same position; it's just taken
us longer to smell the roses. We have operated for nearly forty
years under the assumption that we provided the vast majority
of facilities-related services. Our attention was focused inter-
nally. We used outside contractors only grudgingly. It was not
our intent to overcharge or provide services at what might be
a higher cost, we just thought that we could provide better
services within the constraints of university requirements.
After all, we knew our customers better, or so we thought.

Through the years we would meet at least annually with every
major customer on campus. Our goal was to listen to their
concerns and complaints and provide information on how best
to access our services and on changes in previous requirements
and services. One constant through the years was that the
campus thought that our services cost too much and were not
timely enough. Sound familiar? While we made adjustments
where we could, we just assumed that these demands were not
reasonable. These departments just did not understand what
it cost to maintain and modify institutional type buildings.
They certainly did not know anything about health and safety
codes, building codes, or construction methods. Therefore,
they could not comprehend construction costs. On the other
hand, we did not spend a lot of time comparing how our
competitors were doing business. Our real competitors were
out in the marketplace slugging it out with their competitors.
The better firms gain market share by providing the lowest
prices, highest quality, and the best service, thereby raising the
standard for everyone else. This process never stops. We were
not in the game so we lagged far behind.

Under our newly adopted mission we are comparing many of the services we provide against those offered by outside competitors for price, quality, and service orientation. Our goal has changed from providing the best and lowest cost service by in-house forces to simply providing the best and lowest cost customer required or needed services. We are no longer an employment agency with lifetime guaranteed employment for all our employees. We still value our in-house workforce and will do whatever we can to compete with outside firms. However, the bottom line is that our survival depends on providing a quality service at a competitive cost.

To this end we have started to compare our costs, not simply with other universities, but with our local private competition. The process, commonly referred to as benchmarking, required us to compare our costs, service levels, and quality with others providing the same type of service. In essence, we must act like a business and compete for our customers. As a business competing for campus business, we have a number of advantages, including

1. We know (or should know) our customers needs better.
2. We understand the university environment and should be able to work within its confines better than our outside competitors.
3. We are already on site, so our overhead should be lower. We do not lose time, or as much time, getting to the job, we do not have to advertise, etc.
4. We do not have to make a profit or pay income tax.
5. We have a workforce that already knows the campus.
6. We can choose what work we will contract out.

On the other hand, we have some disadvantages that we must overcome. These include;

1. The campus may have a higher expectation for our work than for that of a contractor.
2. University constraints may impose costs that outside firms may not have to deal with (hiring, firing, and other personnel costs, purchasing costs, high benefits, etc.).
3. Our workforce is conditioned to a noncompetitive environment.

4. Government and/or governing body rules limit management decisions and flexibility.

Even with these problems, we have the opportunity to make
changes.

Quality

Quality can be defined in many ways.   It may refer to a
characteristic, character, or nature. From our perspective, the
real judges of quality are our customers. They may be able to
describe it or simply know it when they see it or experience it.

How does one implement a quality program?   According to
J. Edwards Deming, the father of TQM, one does not implement
quality, one simple does it. Quality, then, is not a program.
Rather, it's a process, a culture, a way of doing business. Once
quality is endemic within your culture it will become self-sus-
taining. This is true whether you utilize TQM, BPR, or other
managerial concepts.

To have quality, your organization must recognize the importance of the process and start with the needs of your customers.
You can work within the framework of your existing processes
and improve them or seek breakthroughs by replacing existing
processes with completely new ones.

The funny thing about quality service is that it normally does
not cost any more than mediocre service. But our perception,
both as providers and consumers of services, is it that quality
costs more. Yet the experience of many companies that have
adopted quality ethics is that quality can actually cost less.
What is the cost of sending someone out three times to fix a
problem versus sending them out just once? What is the cost
of dealing with an irate customer because it takes three calls
to get a problem fixed?

Quality cannot simply be mandated by management. It can
only be attained and sustained in a service organization by the
common focus and belief in excellence by all employees within
the organization. This requires a shared vision and employees
who take ownership of their actions.

Employee Empowerment

In our culture, the term "boss" commonly connotes control, direction, and dominance. On one hand, we expect managers to direct and control their employees, and at the same time extract employee initiative. Empowerment encourages the total involvement of the people actually responsible for delivering services to the customers. The employees providing the service normally know the work better than their managers. They live with their job each day and have probably asked themselves why the work is structured the way it is. But they will seldom ask the "why" question or offer suggestions for improvement because they have the impression that it is not their place, or that their input is not wanted. Therefore, we usually do not get the creative energy of our employees. Managers must come to grips with the balancing act of control versus empowerment. They must strike a balance between the managers need to be in command and the employees' need to feel they are part of the decisions. This makes sense but is very intimidating for the boss.

Empowerment is a means to unleash the true power within your employees. It requires an environment that

- Allows the employee enough **authority and responsibility** to carry out their assigned responsibilities.
- Provides for **accountability** in the exercise of employee authority.
- Encourages staff to actively **participate and influence** planning and process decisions.
- Provides **recognition** of contributions.
- **Develops** staff through training to enhance their ability to contribute toward the improvement of the organization.
- **Communicates** what you are trying to accomplish.

Think of your employees as the creative engine of your organization. Seek out their input and ideas. Do not be satisfied with a few hours of labor each day from your employees, expect their creative energy as well.

Your principal responsibility as the leader of your organization or department is to create an environment that allows each individual to work to their potential. To reach their potential, each employee must buy into the "vision" of the organization. Therefore, the environment you seek encourages employees to take ownership of their actions and work output; they must own responsibility for their own performance.

At our campus we are still seeking to change our environment to this end. We have come a long way on our journey, but the end is still not in sight. While we are seeking this change through a TQM format, the essential strategy is employee empowerment. Our employees have received training in problem-solving techniques and group dynamics and have volunteered for focus groups to study and recommend improvements, modifications, and whole-scale changes in procedures, operations, and department organization. At the same time employees have, within certain parameters, been given greater authority to meet customer expectations. This is an evolving process that has required a vast transfer of information about the department, discussions on the vision and mission of the department, and our need to thrive in our environment.

Continuous Improvement

Continuous improvement refers to a synergy within an organization to never be satisfied with the current processes, quality, output, or service levels. It can come in a variety of flavors. It may work within the framework of your existing processes to incrementally enhance them. The Japanese refer to this as *kaizen*, continuous incremental improvement. Or, as in reengineering, discarding existing processes and implementing entirely new ones. It may even involve both flavors.

Whatever the flavor, continuous improvement involves all of the concepts discussed previously: vision, focus on mission, prediction of environmental changes, entrepreneurial spirit, quality culture, empowered employees, benchmarking, etc. It's a never-ending quest that is expected by your customers and sought by your competitors.

These concepts have begun to make profound changes in our organizational culture. The changes thus far are not monumental and the pace is slow, but it is picking up steam. It took us more than forty years to develop the culture we are now determined to modify. These changes may be characterized by our commitment to focus on customer service and needs, provide these services at a competitive price, with a superior quality, and within the time frame needed by our customers. A few specific examples of how our changing culture is changing how we operate include:

1. We are receiving more compliments from our customers on our service and commitment to meeting their needs. This is happening as our budget continues to be reduced. We recognize that there are still many services that our customers want us to provide, but they now realize that we do not have sufficient resources to provide them. This year, with the full support of a faculty-dominated budget committee, recommendations were made and approved to take scarce general operating funds for deferred maintenance, provide maintenance staff for new buildings, and provide funds to enhance custodial services. This happened at a time when the total campus budget was declining. This was a first on our campus. The change in our culture has been noticed and we believe that this resulted in additional resources to support campus needs.

2. In our quest to provide competitive prices and minimize further service reductions, we began for the first time in our history to contract custodial services for one-third of our campus. The savings from this contract allowed plant operations to absorb a 9 percent budget reduction without any loss or degradation of service. And this reduction was on top of a combined 20 percent reduction the prior two years and nearly 50 percent over the past decade. The portion of the campus receiving contract services received the exact level of services as the remainder of the campus. We are even receiving compliments on the contract service. We were able to implement this contract without laying off permanent staff by eliminating part-time and temporary employees. This move to contracted services has produced tradeoffs: satisfied customers but a very unhappy union and concerned employees.

We are still committed to providing services with our in-house personnel, but only where we can be competitive and provide quality services.

3. We have operated for decades on the assumption that a small backlog of customer requested projects was desirable. This backlog allowed us to more efficiently schedule personnel. It also meant that our customers might have to wait months for work to be completed. Our solution (courtesy of Texas A &M and the U. S. military) was to use delivery order contracting. Under this concept, we will utilize a contractor to handle the level of work that we cannot get to within the time required by our customers. This work will be primarily chargeback work. We expect to begin this contract this fall.

4. We have implemented quality teams to suggest solutions to various issues in our physical plant. For many employees this was the first formal opportunity for them to help shape policy, procedures, and work methods within the department. The energy and enthusiasm of the employees on these teams is phenomenal.

These and many other changes are starting to make a difference with the people who really pay the bills, our customers. They will ultimately determine what they need, what our role will be, and the amount of resources we have to provide these services.

To survive, we must be deeply committed to reevaluating the best means to achieve our mission and to reexamine how we manage our operations. It is critical that we seek means to improve our productivity—not simply to survive, but to thrive with fewer available resources. This cannot be done with a business-as-usual mentality. Our experience indicates that a real customer focus, determination to provide competitively priced, high quality services, employee empowerment, and the quest for continuous improvement will allow the facilities department to survive and thrive.

Fiscal Reality at Michigan State University

Ronald T. Flinn

During the 1980s Michigan State University weathered extreme budget woes that resulted in reducing the full-time physical plant staff from 600 to approximately 500. We take exception to the word "rightsizing" because we were already "lean and mean." However, fiscal reality required rapid and significant steps in order to survive. This experience is being shared to assist others who may be faced with the same dilemma.

Michigan State University Profile

Michigan State University, a pioneer land-grant institution, founded in 1855, is located in East Lansing. Student enrollment is approximately 40,000. The curriculum, which originally concentrated on farm science, now includes more than 200 programs of undergraduate and graduate studies in fourteen degree-granting colleges and a research program of nearly 2,000 projects.

The campus at East Lansing has 5,200 acres, with 3,100 of those acres in experimental farms. The remaining acreage consists of the built-up campus, with 19 million square feet of buildings, including residence halls and apartments capable of housing 20,000 people. Steam and electricity for the built-up campus is totally supplied from a central power plant, and the university is self-sufficient in water from deep rock wells.

This case study describes the impact of budget reductions on general fund supported buildings—11 million square feet with a current replacement value of $1 billion.

History of Events

Over the decades, the state of Michigan occasionally experienced budget shortfalls resulting in reduced appropriations to state-supported agencies, including higher education. This phenomenon was usually triggered by poor automobile sales since auto manufacturing was such a large part of the Michigan economy. Traditionally, these periods of reductions would be followed by years of robust auto sales and a "happy days are here again" atmosphere.

During the 1970s, Michigan State University's funding became progressively less adequate as a result of inflation and state appropriations that did not meet the level of support needed. The university reacted to this severe underfunding with large tuition increases and stringent management of internal reallocation of insufficient resources. Along with an occasional budget retrenchment, it was all too common to be underfunded for labor and supplies.

As Michigan State University entered the 1980s, high inflation continued and there was a sharp decline in the Michigan economy. The appropriation for Michigan State University for 1980-81 was 4.3 percent less than for 1979-80. This followed a nine-year period during which the growth of seven of the nine annual state appropriations for the main campus was lower than the rate of inflation. The impact on the physical plant division was a 5 percent base reduction in its 1980-81 allocation. Certain service frequencies were reduced, and expenditures for equipment and vehicles were deferred to cope with the allocation reduction, but there was a general feeling things would improve in a year or so.

In January 1981, however, the status of the state budget was so dire the governor slashed appropriations to many areas, especially higher education. This led to a mid-year cash management plan that withdrew an additional 4.3 percent of the physical plant budget. We were now clearly in emergency mode.

Developing a Plan

Advance notice that a budget cut will be necessary in the next fiscal year allows one time to develop a carefully thought out plan of action. Conversely, a mid-year cash reduction requires quick action, since only six months or fewer are available to bring expenditures in line with the reduced level of funding.

The university called upon the Committee on Academic Environment to review all proposed plans for coping with the financial emergency. From the physical plant point of view, this was beneficial, since any decision to reduce service became a university decision, not a unilateral decision by physical plant.

Knee-Jerk Reactions

In response to the 1980-81 mid-year cash reduction, the physical plant division issued the following statement:

> *Office cleaning will suffer with dusting and cleaning of furniture discontinued, offices will be cleaned and wastebaskets emptied only once per week (wastebaskets will be emptied other days if placed in the corridors); frequency of cleaning many interior areas will be limited to three times per week with major classroom buildings retaining full daily service.*

> *Two senior management positions, one at the AP 17 level, will be eliminated in physical plant; painting of all office interiors will be discontinued; preventive maintenance throughout the university will be reduced or discontinued.*

Budget planning for the 1981-82 fiscal year required a 13.7 percent reduction of the physical plant budget. As difficult as it was to cope with this level of reduction, we were notified early in the 1981-82 fiscal year that the governor was preparing an executive order to further cut all state budgets. In addition, we were told that the forecast of the state budget was such that further executive orders might be required. In fact, three cash management plans were implemented during 1981-82. These three cash reductions withdrew an additional 5 percent from the physical plant budget.

Being hit this hard and this often with budget reductions forced us to act quickly to reduce expenditures accordingly. A vigorous energy management plan was further fine-tuned to achieve as much savings as possible. All levels of service were slashed dramatically. Unorthodox steps were taken—a swimming pool that had only moderate use was shut down; building air conditioning was not started in buildings with operable sash windows; and in buildings with two elevators, one was shut down. These knee-jerk responses certainly got the attention of the campus community and heightened the awareness of the financial emergency facing us.

As one would expect, a great hue and cry erupted regarding the shutting down of various systems and facilities. As we reflected on these protests and analyzed the other service reductions that had been quickly put in place, it became obvious that some needed to be restored. For example, shutting down elevators did not yield a cost savings, and reducing maintenance levels in high voltage electrical systems for any length of time is a very poor practice. Also, exterior doors and lock hardware must be maintained to assure building security. These experiences led us to realize the importance of having guidelines upon which to prioritize the physical plant service.

The University Committee on Academic Environment reviewed the effects of the implemented service reductions and cost-saving steps and issued the following statement:

> Priorities in physical plant maintenance operations focus on the "least long-term damage." The result is emphasis on maintenance to systems, especially energy systems, and on retaining the integrity of structures, particularly safety systems. While these activities are conducted at the expense of more visible maintenance, they are undoubtedly the most cost effective. The UCAE strongly endorses this approach. The management of physical plant maintenance and the results of its operations are impressive. The committee is concerned with the high level of deferred maintenance programmed because of budget cuts; the long-term costs to the integrity of the university's assets may far exceed the short-term savings.

> The percentage of student employment to the total physical plant maintenance has been increasing. Not only does this appear to be cost effective for the university, but it also benefits the students. The committee believes that the employment of students for these activities should be increased.

> On the surface, General Fund dollars are not used for space cleaning maintenance of athletic facilities. The committee believes that every effort should be made to assure that such activities are supported by athletic funds.

The next three fiscal years we experienced additional significant cash reductions (of 9.1 percent, 4 percent, and 3.8
percent, respectively) to the physical plant budget. Fortunately,
early on it was realized that the utility budgets could not be cut
and were exempt. We were also fortunate to continue to be
allocated monies to maintain and operate all new space that
was added.

The management challenge was further exacerbated by continued growth of the campus as shown in Figure 1.

Zero-Based Budget Thinking

After experiencing wave after wave of budget reductions and
cash management plans, we began to realize that we might be
confronting an era of funding for only absolutely essential
services. We came to the conclusion in the custodial area that
essential services are as follows:

1. Lock and unlock the buildings
2. Remove the trash

Figure 1.
Maintenance and Custodial Staffing.

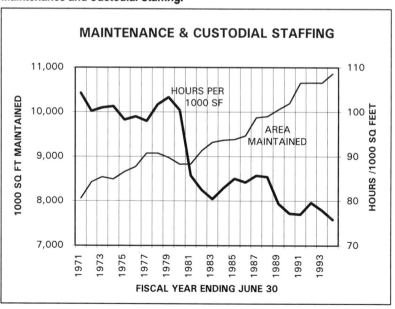

3. Maintain a supply of paper products in the restrooms.

As grim as this thought process is, it does provide an important basis for the developing guidelines to prioritize service responsibilities.

The previous history of events at Michigan State University confirms that a difficult budget situation may very well not be a one-time event, but may continue over several years and require a relatively long-range plan of action. The long-range plan developed at Michigan State University includes the following essential steps:

1. Develop guidelines to prioritize service responsibilities.
2. Accurately identify all activities and associated funding for each service responsibility.
3. Determine the impact to the campus of service reductions in each service area.
4. Communicate effectively with the campus.

Guidelines to Prioritize Service Responsibilities

The challenge normally tossed at the facilities manager is to identify those activities, that, if reduced or eliminated, will produce the least long-range harm to the institution. One of the easiest examples to grasp is that of painting—interior walls do not decay more rapidly for lack of repainting; however, when exterior walls suffer the same neglect, the parent material will quickly deteriorate, requiring replacement at an extremely high cost. After several years of budget cuts, Michigan State University developed guidelines for prioritzing service responsibilities, listed in Figure 2. These guidelines were presented to, and accepted by, its University Committee on Academic Environment.

Identify Each Service Activity and Associated Funding

Each activity performed under each budget must be clearly identified and explained and the associated funding and staffing must be revealed. Admittedly, the effort is arduous and lengthy; however, this is the document upon which all decisions are based, and it must be as accurate as possible. The "All Funds Budget Analysis" is the document developed by MSU

Figure 2.
Guidelines used to prioritize service responsibilities.

> To meet this mission, the division has used, and will continue to use, the following guidelines to prioritize service responsibilities:
>
> - Maintain security and safety systems (door locks, hinges, fire alarms, etc.).
> - Assure reliability of utility systems (heat, electricity, water, gas, and communications).
> - Satisfy codes, laws, and regulations regarding operations, safety, and sanitation.
> - Keep weather out of buildings; maintain roofs, exterior walls, windows, and doors.
> - Avoid reduction of services which would cause property loss; maintain exterior paint, floor finishes, water treatment chemicals, fire sprinklers, etc.
> - Maintain building appurtenances (chalkboards, fixed seating, lighting, etc.) at minimum standards necessary for teaching and research.
> - Maintain energy consuming systems to avoid waste.
> - Maintain minimum occupant comfort and convenience (elevators, air conditioning, etc.).
> - Keep up the appearance of the "campus front door." Entrance lobbies and first floor corridors have priority.

and excerpts detailing the paint budget and custodial budget are displayed in Appendices I and II. Obviously, the "All Funds Budget Analysis" is a voluminous document, but in order to clearly chronicle all the budgeted responsibilities of the physical plant division, it is essential.

Determine Impact of Service Reductions

Once the targeted areas for budget reductions are agreed upon, one needs to state the impact to the campus and reveal the associated budget reductions and staff reductions (see Appendices III and IV). Obviously, a summary of all proposed budget reductions should also be presented (see Appendix V).

At MSU, the decision was made up front that the university budget for providing heat, cooling, and lights would not be subject to budget reductions. Central administration mounted a campaign to persuade the campus community to be frugal and prudent in its use of such utilities.

Communicate with Campus

With luck, the budget cutting is campus-wide and not just focused on the support service areas. Faculty and staff not actively involved in the budget-cutting process are somewhat oblivious to it and are shocked or surprised when service reductions such as cutbacks in custodial services directly affect them. It is not uncommon for physical plant to be accused of singling out a college or department, or grandstanding in an attempt to protect its budget. One of the most effective ways to paint a true picture of the situation is to communicate with the entire campus community through articles in the student newspaper or campus news bulletin, but experience has shown a direct mailing is at times necessary. Examples are included in Appendix VI.

It is essential the entire physical plant staff fully understands the facts regarding the service reductions. In discussions with other members of the campus community, staff must convey that the service reductions were a campus-wide determination, not a unilateral decision on the part of the physical plant division.

It has also been found effective to quickly orient an audience to the impact of repeated budget cuts by presenting the story on one sheet of paper (Appendix VII). For other audiences, an executive summary is appropriate (Appendix VIII).

Conclusion

Clearly, a forced rightsizing by budget reductions is not an exercise one looks forward to; however, there are some silver linings in the dark clouds.

- All leaders in the facilities management area become very cognizant of the functional activities of the unit and how much of the budget is allocated to those activities.

- It provides a window of opportunity to reorganize, and there is an increased willingness on the part of the workforce and supervisors to be agreeable when they realize it will enhance job security; i.e., transfer of skilled trades employees from Maintenance assignments to the Alterations and Improvement crew.

- It causes the organization to recognize the need to have "the best out of everyone" and allows for the introduction of unorthodox programs of incentives and rewards that previously were thought to be unnecessary. This improved productivity obviously is part of any "quality" program. Increasing training to its maximum level of effectiveness must also be implemented.

- Innovative ideas are more readily accepted and implemented. Employee groups and unions appear more willing to listen to less traditional ideas, perhaps some that may have seemed threatening in the past; i.e., the use of student workers to supplement the workforce.

- Appreciation for the support service staff rises across campus.

Appendix I

Administrative Unit: Physical Plant
Department: Maintenance Services
Program Name: Paint

All Funds Budget Analysis

1980-81 Budget 472,500 X
1981-82 Base Reduction Plan

Program Description	Detail Expenditure Item	FTE	Budget Amount	Account Gen. Fund	Number Other
1. Glass Replacement and Glazing. This function covers window and mirror glass replacement and reglazing. This include 28,700,000 square feet of glass in 44,000 windows,555 restroom mirrors and tempered safety glass for all doors. Considerable effort is expended in the reglazing of all Greenhouses which are a constant maintenance problem because of the high humidity. Prompt replacement of glass is necessary for building security, energy conservation and in many cases personnel safety. Reglazing is performed to minimize energy loss through infiltration and reduce damage cause by water penetration.	Labor - Glazers Supplies	1.0	19,800 40,800	11-5202 11-5203	
2. Exterior Painting. This function provides protective coatings, on a 8 year cycle, to over 3 million square feet of exposed non-masonry exterior surfaces ranging from window frames, trim and door finishing on the main campus to complete structures in the rural area. Exterior railings are also maintained in accordance with CSHA safety standard color codes. Failure to maintain exterior painting will allow more rapid deterioration of building surfaces and will result in the replacement of window sills, door frames, etc.	Labor - Painters Supplies	6.9	131,500 21,900	11-5202 11-5203	
3. Shades, Blinds and Awnings. This function is responsible for the repair and replacement of 9,600 venetian blinds, 2,000 window shades and 270 exterior awnings on campus which provides control of natural light.	Supplies		5,000	11-5203	
4. Interior Painting. This function provides for the refinishing of 30 million square feet of interior surfaces on a cycle of 20 years, using some 13,500 gallons of paint, varnish and lacquer. Wall fabrics, covering 400,000 square feet, are also maintained in areas where structural movement has caused maintenance problems or where surfaces are exposed to excessive wear. In compliance with OSHA standards, all fire doors and wall panel boxes, such as fire boxes and electrical and telephone panels, are being color coded as buildings are being repainted. The 20 year paint cycle has generated considerable criticism from campus occupants.	Labor - Painter - Tradeshelpers Supplies Equipment (for the above)	5.5 1.9	104,700 28,500 87,300 1,000	11-5202 11-5202 11-5203 11-5204	
5. Customer Work Orders. Activities performed by physical Plant with reimbursements by the customer.	Labor	7.2	122,900		Various
6. Supervision and Coordination. This function covers supervision, procurement, planning, and inspection for the above activities and responsibility for the productivity of the workforce.	Salary - Supervisor SS-55 - Coordinator 2 CT-12	1.0 .5	21,000 11,000	11-5202 11-5202	

Appendix II

Administrative Unit Physical Plant

Department   Custodial Services

Program Name

All Funds **Budget Analysis**

Page 1 of 5

1980-81 Budget 3,791,708 X

1981-82 Base Reduction Plan

Program Description	Detail Expenditure Item	FTE	Budget Amount	Account Gen. Fund	Number Other
General custodial service is performed to keep buildings at a safe and acceptable standard. Health and safety guidelines are incorporated with the department standards to form the performance criteria. Custodial tasks are performed on a "as necessary" basis such as daily, semiweekly, weekly, quarterly, or yearly. Each FTE is responsible for servicing approximately 28,000 square feet.					
1. Restrooms (700) - floors are dust mopped daily and wet mopped in wet weather and disinfected weekly. The floors are also stripped and sealed 4 times a year. All enamel, including commodes, urinals and sinks are cleaned and sanitized daily. Mirrors are cleaned daily and doors and partitions are wiped down weekly. All horizontal surfaces such as window sills and heating convertors are dusted weekly. All waste receptacles are emptied daily. Restrooms are restocked using 120,000 rolls of toilet tissue, 48,000 rolls of paper towels, 22,000 bars of soap and 5,000 sponges annually.	Labor - Custodial Workers Supplies	26	304,928 88,000	11-5032 11-5033	
2. Shower areas (370) - all floors are cleaned and sanitized twice a week. The floors are stripped and sealed 3 times a year. All fixtures, walls and ceilings are kept free of dirt, bacteria and lime buildup and replenished with soap. All waste receptacles are emptied daily. Horizontal surfaces such as window sills and heating convertors are cleaned weekly.	Labor - Custodial Workers Supplies	6	70,368 4,000	11-5032 11-5033	
3. Locker Rooms (80) - floors are clean and disinfected daily and the floors are stripped and sealed 3 times a year. Water fountains and waste baskets are cleaned daily and all horizontal surfaces such as window sills, locker tops, benches and heating convertors are dusted weekly.	Labor - Custodial Workers Supplies	12	140,736 4,000	11-5032 11-5033	
4. Classrooms (450) - hard surface floors, wood, tile and terrazzo are dust mopped daily and ruing wet weather are wet mopped daily. Carpeted floors are vacuumed twice a week and shampooed yearly. Wood and terrazzo floors are stripped and resealed yearly, tile floors are stripped and refinished approximately three times a year. Horizontal surfaces such as window sills, desks, chairs and heating convertors are dusted weekly. Chalkboards and erasers are washed and cleaned daily, supplies replenished and wastebaskets are emptied daily. Spills or accidents resulting in soil to building surfaces are cleaned as necessary.	Labor - Custodial Workers Supplies	62	727,136 34,000	11-5032 11-5033	

Administrative Unit __Physical Plant__
Department __Custodial Services__
Program Name __

All Funds Budget Analysis
Page 2 of 5

1980-81 Budget ____
1981-82 Base Reduction Plan ____

	Program Description	Detail Expenditure Item	FTE	Budget Amount	Account Gen. Fund	Number Other
5.	Laboratories (1,484) - floors are dust mopped twice a week and during wet weather are wet mopped daily or as needed. Wood and terrazzo floors are stripped and resealed yearly, tile floors are stripped and refinished approximately three times a year. Horizontal surfaces such as window sills, desks, chairs and heating convertors are dusted weekly. Chalkboards and erasers are washed and cleaned daily, supplies replenished and wastebaskets are emptied daily, supplies replenished and wastebaskets are emptied daily. Spills or accidents resulting in soil to building surfaces are cleaned as necessary. Sinks are cleaned as requested and labs are stocked with towels.	Labor - Custodial Workers Supplies	30	351,840 40,000	11-5032 11-5033	
6.	Servicemen - this function provides the unlocking and locking of all exterior doors of assigned buildings seven days a week as posted or scheduled. They are also assigned to police circulation areas in all buildings, checking toilets for supplies and cleanliness. They also keep entrances clear in inclement weather shoveling, sweeping and vacuuming as necessary for pedestrian safety. They also respond to emergencies such as spills resulting from accidents or sickness.	Labor - Custodial Workers Supplies	7	82,096 3,000	11-5032 11-5033	
7.	Public circulation areas in all academic and office buildings receive daily care. Hard surface floors, wood, tile and terrazzo are dust mopped daily and during wet weather are wet mopped daily. Wood and terrazzo floors are stripped and resealed yearly or more often if necessary. Tile floors are stripped and refinished approximately three times a year. Circulation areas that are carpeted are vacuumed daily or as necessary and shampooed at least yearly or more often. Horizontal surfaces such as window sills, tables, desks and heating convertors are dusted weekly and waste is taken care of daily.	Labor - Custodial Workers Supplies	20	234,560 24,000	11-5032 11-5033	
8.	Certain buildings require additional custodial services due to extended hours, high usage and activities seven days a week. These buildings are the Library, I.M. Sports Circle and I.M. West. The restrooms, shower rooms, locker rooms and gym areas are cleaned daily and the high traffic areas, entryways and steps of these buildings receive attention for cleanliness and safety.	Labor - Custodial Workers	3	35,184	11-5032	

Administrative Unit Physical Plant
Department Custodial Services
Program Name _____

All Funds **Budget Analysis**
Page 3 of 5

1980-81 Budget _____
1981-82 Base Reduction Plan _____

	Program Description	Detail Expenditure Item	FTE	Budget Amount	Account Gen. Fund	Number Other
9.	Clinical Center - all tiled floor surfaces in patient areas are mopped daily with disinfectant in addition to normal dust mopping. Mops are changed daily (individual mop for each module) and require additional laundry expense. Approximately 1,300 pieces of furniture and equipment are cared for, inspected and disinfected daily if used. All stainless steel door plates, light switches and kick plates are washed and disinfected daily. Trash removal from all treatment rooms is treated separately and the waste containers receive new plastic liners daily. Occasionally, where patients with highly contagious disease are treated a fogging machine is used to apply disinfectant; the room is completely sealed off, all equipment covered and when room is reopened all furniture is wiped down and the floor is mopped.	Labor - Custodial Workers Supplies	6	70,368 7,000	11-5032 11-5033	
10.	Veterinary clinic receives additional services beyond general custodial care. Surgery, examination and waiting rooms and equipment have to be sanitized and the floors mopped with disinfectant.	Labor - Custodial Workers Supplies	1	11,728 1,500	11-5032 11-5033	
11.	At Fee Hall the Carcinogenics floor area receives additional care due to the need of a dust free area.	Labor - Custodial Workers Supplies	.5	5,864 500	11-5032 11-5033	
12.	Offices (5,000) - hard surface floors, wood, tile and terrazzo are dust mopped twice a week and wet mopped daily where necessary in wet weather. Carpeted floors are vacuumed twice a week and shampooed yearly. Wood and terrazzo floors are stripped and resealed.	Labor - Custodial Workers Supplies	70	829,688 40,000	11-5032 11-5033	
13.	Lights are services as necessary on a failure basis and fixtures are cleaned and dusted at this time. This task requires approximately 25,000 bulbs and tubes annually. Tubes and bulbs are funded through the electrical account.	Labor - Custodial Workers Supplies	6	70,368	11-5032 11-5043	
14.	Swimming pool operators - this function provides the cleaning of the four indoor pools and pool areas daily and the outdoor pool and pool areas daily plus the outdoor pool when operating; they also clean the outdoor pool and pool area each spring prior to pool opening; operate the water treatment equipment, take water samples; perform and record required water and chlorination tests for Department of Public Health; perform minor maintenance to the pool water supply and recirculation equipment and service water softening equipment in buildings with pools.	Labor - Custodial Workers Supplies	4	46,912 40,000	11-5032 11-5033	

Administrative Unit __Physical Plant__
Department __Custodial Services__
Program Name__

All Funds Budget Analysis
Page 4 of 5

1980-81 Budget _____
1981-82 Base Reduction Plan_____

Program Description	Detail Expenditure Item	FTE	Budget Amount	Account Gen. Fund	Number Other
15. Gymnasiums, hand ball and squash courts and dance studio floors are dust mopped daily and wet mopped weekly. Gymnasium and dance floors are cleaned and refinished yearly. Bleacher seating, window sills and convertors are dusted weekly. Drinking fountains and other enamel are cleaned daily and all waste receptacles are emptied daily.	Labor - Custodial Workers Supplies	2 1	70,368 4,000	11-5032 11-5033	
16. Operation of the Auditorium and Fairchild stage - this function is managed by the Custodial Department and is responsible for all stage activities and the operation of lighting, sound and special effects equipment. The Custodial Department is responsible for equipment safety and repair of the stage, lighting, curtain switchboards, and sound equipment, projection equipment and appurtenances; also schedules part-time employees, hires and supervises stagehands and schedules needed equipment and cleaning.	Funded by activities on Fairchild and Auditorium stages	1.5	27,788		21-2906
17. Set-up crew - this function provides setups required by special needs for orientation, registration, graduation, etc. and includes obtaining and setting of tables, chairs and related furniture. They also do special setups for football, basketball, hockey and other sports performing such assignments as transporting and setting bleachers, basketball floors and related athletic equipment. They perform departmental requests for moves on campus plus needed labor services. All cleaning before, during and after the above described events are performed also by the set up crew. This service is performed on request only and is paid for by the customer.	Customer Work Orders Sporting Events, Registration, Graduation, etc. Departmental Moves Supplies	6 3 3	96,000 48,000 48,000 192,000 10,000		Various
18. Supervision - a manager, 12 supervisors and a training coordinator direct the Custodial Services Division. The staff consists of 295 FTE positions (232 full-time employees and 126 part-time student employees). Supervision directs and controls the custodial work force in all assigned duties. The training coordinator shows new personnel how to use equipment and products correctly and handles retraining of employees when new equipment and products are used. The training coordinator interviews and holds orientation for new employees, updates and implements the shift preference list, performs building inspections, keeps inventory of all cleaning equipment, purchases supplies and equipment, prepares postings for new and vacated positions and tests new materials and equipment.	AP14 AP13 AP11 S33 S55	1 1 2 9 1	31,000 25,296 48,417 153,740 20,500	11-5031 11-5031 11-5031 11-5032 11-5032	

Administrative Unit Physical Plant
Department Custodial Services
Program Name

All Funds Budget Analysis
Page 5 of 5

1980-81 Budget
1981-82 Base Reduction Plan

Program Description	Detail Expenditure Item	FTE	Budget Amount	Account Gen. Fund	Account Other	Number
19. Office Services - three persons perform the necessary secretarial and clerical tasks. Two on the day shift and one on the afternoon shift. They handle room reservations, personnel records, payroll distribution, worker's compensation cases, requisitions, purchase orders, typing and miscellaneous records, receive and transmit departmental maintenance and dumpster calls and other radio messages and perform other tasks as required by the Custodial Services Department.	Office Ass't II / Clerical	2 / 1	28,995 / 9,500	11-5031 / 11-5031		
20. Equipment - the Custodial Department has approximately 500 pieces of motorized floor care equipment such as buffers, automatic scrubbers, water vacs and vacuum cleaners. These units have an average life expectancy of 14 years and therefore requires replacement of 36 units per year. Equipment budget needs to be increased to $30,000 annually.	Equipment		5,500	11-5034		
21. Stockroom - two people receive and issue stock and uniforms. Among the items handled are 5,875 gallons of floor cleaners, finishers, detergents, soaps, carpet shampoos and ammonia; also the paper products and small equipment are distributed through the stockroom. Uniforms for employees are distributed and collected weekly and minor maintenance is performed on custodial equipment and building distribution facilities.	Stockroom Attendant / Labor Custodial Worker / Supplies	1 / 1	14,248 / 11,728 / 3,000	11-5032 / 11-5032 / 11-5033		
22. Venetian blinds (268,300 sq. ft.) are laundered on four year cycle. At the time of laundering any necessary repairs are also performed to assure safe and efficient operation of the blinds.	Supplies		25,000	11-5033		
23. Windows (42,000) interior and exterior windows are washed yearly.	Labor Custodial Workers / Supplies	5	58,640 / 4,000	11-5032 / 11-5033		

Appendix III

Michigan State University

MAJOR ADMINISTRATIVE UNIT_____ Physical Plant

1980-81 SPENDING REDUCTION PLAN

1982-82 BASE BUDGET REDUCTION PLAN ___115,000 (Labor - $75,000; S&S $40,000)

UNIT OR ACTIVITY ____Paint Maintenance & Repair

ACCOUNT NUMBER 11 - 520_____

Item/Action Taken or Planned	Effective Date	Fiscal Year Savings or Base Reduction	Impact
Discontinue replacement of vinyl wallcoverings. Patch and repair only.	80-81	2,000 Labor 4,000 Supplies	Interior less attractive -0.1 regular employee
Discontinue painting office interiors. Restrict classroom and public areas to one coat with no color changes.	80-81	22,000 Labor 8,000 Supplies	Interior less attractive -1.3 regular employees
Reduce classroom and public area painting to repair of damaged areas and touch up. In effect this eliminates the remaining scheduled repainting program for interiors.	81-82	51,000 Labor 28,000 Supplies	Interior less attractive -3.0 regular employees

Appendix IV

Michigan State University

MAJOR ADMINISTRATIVE UNIT_____ <u>Physical Plant</u>

1980-81 SPENDING REDUCTION PLAN

1982-82 BASE BUDGET REDUCTION PLAN __<u>582,508 (Labor - $540,008; Supplies 42,500)</u>

UNIT OR ACTIVITY ___<u>Custodial</u>_____

ACCOUNT NUMBER 11 - <u>503</u>_____

Item/Action Taken or Planned	Effective Date	Fiscal Year Savings or Base Reduction	Impact
1. Reduce restroom cleaning of enamel and mirrors in 200 restrooms to M-W-F. Supplies will be replenished and waste removed daily. Balance of approximately 355 restrooms in heavy traffic classroom buildings will retain daily service.	80-81 81-82	35,000 Labor 50,000 Supplies	Lower cleaning standards. -6 regular and -3 student employees
2. Reduce frequency of shower area cleaning approximately 16%.	81-82	12,000 Labor	Lower cleaning standards. -1 regular employee
3. In locker rooms, scrubbing and sealing of floors will be reduced from 3 times a year to twirce a year. General cleaning frequency will be reduced 20%.	81-82	24,000 Labor	Lower cleaning standards. -2 regular employees
5. Reduce cleaning in Bioresearch to four hours per day.	80-81 81-82	3,000 Labor 3,000 Labor	Adjusting irregular to regular schedule -0.5 regular employee

Michigan State University

MAJOR ADMINISTRATIVE UNIT_____ Physical Plant

1980-81 SPENDING REDUCTION PLAN

1982-82 BASE BUDGET REDUCTION PLAN _____

UNIT OR ACTIVITY _____ Custodial (con't) _____

ACCOUNT NUMBER 11 - 503____

Item/Action Taken or Planned	Effective Date	Fiscal Year Savings or Base Reduction	Impact
5. Reduce rural building cleaning to four hours a day (Observatory, Dairy Research, Endocrine Lab., Beef Cattle Reesearch & Purebred Cattle Teaching Center).	80-81 81-82	35,000 Labor 50,000 Supplies	Reduce cleaning frequency -0.5 regular employee
5. Reduction of service to other laboratories.	81-82	15,000 Labor	Lower cleaning standards. -1 regular employee
6. Reduce service employees from 3 to 2 for weekend cleaning & unlocking; also reduce daytime rover cleaning service employees from 7 to 5.	80-81 81-82	10,000 Labor 24.000 Labor	Results in less special cleaning service on weekends and during week
8. Library (stack area) - reduce cleaning to once a week, except 1st floor.	80-81 81-82	9,000 Labor 9,000 Labor	Lower cleaning standards. -1 regular employee and -1.5 student employees
9. Eliminate funding of extra custodial service to Clinical Center.	81-82	70,368 Labor 6,500 Supplies	Cost to be reimbursed by Clinical Center
12. Discontinue dusting & cleaning of office furniture.	80-81 81-82	36,000 Labor 36,000 Labor	Lower cleaning standards. -6 regular employees

Michigan State University

MAJOR ADMINISTRATIVE UNIT_____ Physical Plant

1980-81 SPENDING REDUCTION PLAN

1982-82 BASE BUDGET REDUCTION PLAN _____

UNIT OR ACTIVITY _____ Custodial (con't)_____

ACCOUNT NUMBER 11 - 503_____

Item/Action Taken or Planned	Effective Date	Fiscal Year Savings or Base Reduction	Impact
Clean offices and empty wastebaskets once a week. Empty wastebaskets on othe days only when places incorridor by the office occupant.	80-81 81-82	50,000 Labor 50,000 Supplies	Lower cleaning standards -5 regular employee and -14 student employees
14,. close one circle IM indoor pool and West IM outdoor pool.	81-82	8,000 Labor 6,500 Supplies	Old pool at Circle IM is seldom used. Would eliminate swimming at outdoor pool. -.75 regular employee
15. Reduce general custodial care to gymnasiums, handball, squash courts and dance floors.	81-82	12,000 Labor	Lower cleaning standards -1.0 regular employee
18. Reduce overtime for nine supervisors.	80-81 81-82	12,000 Labor 7,000 Labor	Procedural change
22. Suspend venetian blind cleaning for 81-82.	81-82	25,000 Supplies	Lower cleaning standards
23. Suspend all window washing for 81-82.	81-82	58,649 Labor 4,000 Supplies	Film and dust will remain unless occupants clean their own windows -5.0 regular employees

Appendix V

SUMMARY OF PHYSICAL PLANT BUDGET REDUCTION PLAN

Unit	80-81 Budget	15% of Budget	Proposed Reduction	% Reduction
Administration	$ 276,274	$ 41,441	$ 15,000	5.4%[1]
Special	140,413	21,062	71,790	51.3%
Custodial	3,791,708	568,756	582,508	15.4%
Electrical	733,500	110,025	79,000	10.8%[2]
HVAC Operations	628,000	94,200	50,000	8.0%[2]
Mechanical	534,700	80,205	24,000	4.5%[2]
Maintenance Supv.	360,355	54,053	21,000	5.8%
Paint	472,500	70,875	115,000	24.3%
Plumbing	354,300	53,145	25,000	7.1%[2]
Structural	665,700	99,855	106,000	15.9%
Engineering	175,000	26,250	27,000	15.4%
Telephones	117,811	17,672	117,811	100.0%[3]
Truck Replacement	45,000	6,750	10,000	22.2%
Total	$8,295,261	$1,244,289	$1,244,289	15.0%

1. This reduction is in addition to a 13% or $36,000 reduction taken at beginning of 80-81 by eliminating an A-P 17 position.

2. Codes, regulations, safety, reliability and energy conservation precludes additional reduction.

3. Telephone account discontinued during 80-81.

NOTE: The identification number of the various items on the attached pages will refer the reader back to the proper activity on the program statement.

Appendix VI

MICHIGAN STATE UNIVERSITY

PHYSICAL PLANT DIVISION
PHYSICAL PLANT BUILDING

EAST LANSING • MICHIGAN 48824-1215
TELEPHONE • 517 355-3366
FAX • 517 353-6358

January 16, 1989

MEMORANDUM

TO: Deans, Directors, Chairpersons, Heads of Administrative Units

FROM: R. T. Flinn

SUBJECT: **Physical Plant Service Reductions**

Recent inquiries and expressions of concern, regarding the latest Physical Plant Service cutbacks, confirm the need to clarify the current service level authorized by the General Fund.

In keeping with the intent of Refocusing, Rebalancing and Refining (R^3), the Physical Plant Division has used, and will continue to use, the following guidelines to prioritize service responsibilities:

- ○ *Maintain security and safety systems (door locks, hinges, fire alarms, etc.).*
- ○ *Assure reliability of utility systems (heat, electricity, water, gas, and communications).*
- ○ *Satisfy codes, laws, and regulations regarding operations, safety, and sanitation.*
- ○ *Keep weather out of buildings; maintain roofs, exterior walls, windows and doors.*
- ○ *Avoid reduction of services which would cause property loss; maintain exterior paint, floor finishes, water treatment chemicals, fire sprinklers, etc..*
- ○ *Maintain building appurtenances (chalkboards, fixed seating, lighting, etc.) at minimum standards necessary for teaching and research.*
- ○ *Maintain energy consuming systems to avoid waste.*
- ○ *Maintain minimum occupant comfort and convenience (elevators, air conditioning, etc.).*
- ○ *Keep up the appearance of the "campus front door" - entrance lobbies and first floor corridors have priority.*

Two attachments itemize the more significant services, those having direct impact upon campus constituents, which have been eliminated or reduced in Custodial Services and Maintenance Services. These service reductions began in 1980-81 with the University's Budget Adjustment Plan. All General Fund activities were reviewed, and service levels were adjusted in a manner to have the least long-range impact upon the institution. It is important to recognize that these Physical Plant service reductions have come on top of a funding level which is the lowest in the Big 10 and one of the lowest in the nation.

An additional 10 to 15% cut, during the next three to four years, is in the planning process. Budget cuts of this magnitude, and the resulting service reductions, will have an enormous impact upon the campus academic and physical environment. We would appreciate ideas on how best to face the financial dilemma without irrevocably harming the University's mission.

RTF/dd
Attachments

CUSTODIAL SERVICES DEPARTMENT
PHYSICAL PLANT DIVISION
MICHIGAN STATE UNIVERSITY

SERVICES ELIMINATED:

- dusting and cleaning of office furniture
- cleaning of Venetian blinds
- washing of windows
* - weekend service to Intramural buildings
* - classroom clean up after snow season

SERVICES REDUCED:

- reduce daily cleaning of public circulation areas to 2 times per <u>week</u>, except in first floor area
- reduce classroom dustmopping from daily to every other day
- reduce frequency of wet mopping of classrooms to twice weekly
- reduce cleaning of enamel surfaces and mirrors in restrooms to M-W-F
- reduce scrubbing and sealing of locker room floors from 3 times per year to 2 times per year
- reduce dustmopping of laboratories to once per week
* - reduce office cleaning from <u>once per week</u> to <u>twice monthly</u> (wastebaskets will be emptied only if place in hallway)
* - routine replacement of burned out fluorescent and/or incandescent lamps to <u>twice monthly</u>
* - stripping/scrubbing of resilient floors will be completed <u>during summer only</u>

For additional information, please call Custodial Services (5-8485).

* New item or modification of item listed on previous communication dated February 27, 1987.

rtfcs3
12/5/88

MAINTENANCE SERVICES DEPARTMENT
PHYSICAL PLANT DIVISION
MICHIGAN STATE UNIVERSITY

SERVICES ELIMINATED:

- painting of office interiors
* - replacement of any chalkboards or bulletin boards
- clock re-setting
- replacement of leaking and discolored thermopane windows
* - repairs to window shades and Venetian blinds
* - repairs to refrigerated water coolers
* - maintenance of all master clock systems; remove on failure
* - replacement of cracked window glass; replace only if missing
* - replacement of missing or broken floor cove base
* - cleaning, lubricating and functional checks of high voltage switchgear

SERVICES REDUCED:

- repairs to painting in classrooms and public circulation areas is limited to touch-up of damaged surfaces
- repairs to interior walls, floors and ceilings
- repairs to lighting fixtures and electrical circuits
- repairs to plumbing, heating, ventilation, and air conditioning systems
- repairs to damaged doors, windows, and screens
* - repairs to fixed classroom and auditorium seating; inspection cycle extended to 2.5 years, remove broken seats, batch repair
- frequency of roof inspections
* - frequency of building plumbing inspections extended from 30 to 36 months
* - replacement of improper fitting doors and windows
* - water softener maintenance, reduce regenerations from 4 to 6 weeks
* - maintenance on low voltage electrical system, lighting systems and elevator equipment
* - daily maintenance of of absorption air conditioning systems
* - repair and calibration of pneumatic and electric control systems
* - scheduled preventative maintenance of steam distribution, system, HVAC systems, pumps and air compressors, building perimeter heating systems
* - cleaning of storm and sanitary sewers

For additional information, please call Maintenance Services (3-1760).

* New item or modification of item listed on previous communication dated February 27, 1987.

rtfms3
12/5/88

Appendix VII

**SIGNIFICANT BUDGET REDUCTIONS IN CUSTODIAL AND MAINTENANCE ACTIVITIES
SINCE JULY 1, 1980***

CUSTODIAL
Venetian Blind Cleaning	100.0%
Window Washing	100.0
Dusting and Cleaning of Office Furniture	100.0
Office Cleaning	57.9
Additional Service to Buildings with Extended Hours	46.4
Service Workers - Unlockers & Day Custodians	34.5
Restroom Cleaning	22.0
Classroom Cleaning	8.7

ELECTRICAL
Clock Resetting & Maint.	100.0%
Building Lighting Fixtures	52.9
Building Low Voltage Systems	43.0
Motors & Controls	37.9
Street & Walkway Lighting	31.6

HVAC
Refrigerated Water Cooler Maint.	100.0%
Heat, Vent & Air Conditioning Systems	64.5

MECHANICAL
Building Perimeter Heating Systems	45.4%

GLASS REGLAZING & PAINT
Replacement of Leaking & Discolored Thermopane Windows	100.0%
Interior Painting	100.0
Greenhouse Reglazing	50.0

PLUMBING
Operation & Maint. of Water Softeners	100.0%
Plumbing Faucet & Valve Repair	31.8
Storm & Sanitary Sewers	30.0

STRUCTURAL
Toilet Partition Door Hardware	100.0%
Window Shade, Blinds and Sun Screen Repairs	100.0
Interior door closers	100.0
Walls, Floors & Ceiling Repairs	66.2
Fixed Classroom &Auditorium Seating	59.0

AVERAGE ALL ACTIVITIES
Custodial Services	29.0%
Maintenance Services	22.0

*As a Percent of 80-81 Budget Base in 1992-93 dollars   AC/rtfreduc 3/10/93

Appendix VIII

MICHIGAN STATE UNIVERSITY
1993-94 SUPPORT SERVICES PROGRAM PLANNING AND REVIEW

PHYSICAL PLANT DIVISION
EXECUTIVE SUMMARY

UNIT MISSION

The mission of the Physical Plant Division is to provide and maintain the physical environment conducive for education, research and public service at Michigan State University.

GUIDELINES USED TO PRIORITIZE SERVICE RESPONSIBILITIES

To meet this mission, the Division has used, and will continue to use, the following guidelines to prioritize service responsibilities:

- *Maintain security and safety systems (door locks, hinges, fire alarms, etc.).*
- *Assure reliability of utility systems (heat, electricity, water, gas, and communications).*
- *Satisfy codes, laws and regulations regarding operations, safety and sanitation.*
- *Keep weather out of buildings; maintain roofs, exterior walls, windows and doors.*
- *Avoid reduction of services which would cause property loss; maintain exterior paint, floor finishes, water treatment chemicals, fire sprinklers, etc.*
- *Maintain building appurtenances (chalkboards, fixed seating, lighting, etc.) at minimum standards necessary for teaching and research.*
- *Maintain energy consuming systems to avoid waste.*
- *Maintain minimum occupant comfort and convenience (elevators, air conditioning, etc.).*
- *Keep up the appearance of the "campus front door"; entrance lobbies and first floor corridors have priority.*

SERVICES ELIMINATED AND REDUCED

Since 1980-81, the Division's budgets have been cut $5,222,000 (26%) in 1992-93 dollars. Custodial cuts total 29% and Maintenance cuts 22%. Supervisory and support staff have been reduced accordingly.

CUSTODIAL SERVICES:

ELIMINATED: *Washing windows, cleaning blinds, dusting office furniture, weekend I.M. building service, special classroom cleanup after snow season, policing of classrooms and teaching labs.*

REDUCED: *Offices now cleaned quarterly, laboratories weekly, public areas three times a week, classrooms every other day, chalkboards three times weekly. Waste baskets emptied if set in hall. Slow replacement of burned-out lights. Floors are stripped and scrubbed only once a year. Carpet is shampooed only once a year.*

MAINTENANCE SERVICES:

ELIMINATED: *All interior painting, clock resetting, operation and repair of water softeners, repair of water coolers, master clock systems, cracked windows, shades, blinds, sun screens, damaged toilet partitions, and damaged or missing ceiling tiles and floor cove base. Repair or replacement of defective automatic door closers except as required by fire code.*

REDUCED: *Heating and air conditioning repairs - more "too hot/cold" complaints;*
Repair of defective elevators, light fixtures and circuits - increased disruption;
Plumbing fixture maintenance - slower response;
Repair of walls, ceilings, floors, doors, and windows - patching only the critical.

INCREASED WORKLOAD

New building space of 1,853,000 square feet (+21%) has increased cleaning and maintenance work loads while full-time staff has been reduced 18% or 80 positions -- 45 in Custodial Services alone. Not surprisingly, MSU is one of the lowest funded Physical Plant operations in the nation and *the lowest in the Big Ten*.

The Division also assumed expanded responsibility for the MSU utility bill. In the mid-eighties, Physical Plant accepted responsibility for managing internal utility billing to auxiliary services of $5,650,000 per year -- with no staff additions. In 1987, responsibility for $250,000 of "farm area" utility bills was also assumed.

Recent governmental regulations regarding PCBs (polychlorinated biphenyls) in electrical transformers, lead in drinking water, asbestos abatement, Right-To-Know, underground storage tanks, and ADA as well as "Sick Building Syndrome" concerns, etc., have required costly surveys and reporting systems as well as increased costs of performing routine maintenance.

FUNDING PRIORITIES AND PROGRAMMATIC CHANGES ANTICIPATED

Following the priorities stated above, additional 10% and 20% reductions will result in:

> ADMINISTRATION AND ENGINEERING
> - *Significantly slower administrative response.*
> - *Lower ability to absorb emergency repairs.*

> CUSTODIAL SERVICES
> - *Ability to provide only basic services - locking and unlocking buildings, replenishing restroom paper products, removing trash placed in hallways.*
> - *Classrooms and public areas being filthy and trash laden.*
> - *Floor surfaces eroding for lack of protective coating and proper cleaning.*
> - *Morale, and productivity, plummeting due to intolerable work loads of 50,000 square feet per employee -- 2.5 times national standards.*

> MAINTENANCE SERVICES
>
> | | |
> |---|---|
> | Electrical Repair: | - *Failed light fixtures and equipment will remain unserviced for extended periods.* |
> | | - *Elevators will be tagged out of service until reduced repair crews can respond.* |
> | HVAC & Mechanical: | - *Heating, ventilating and air conditioning equipment will remain out of service for lengthy periods. Building occupants will occasionally go home.* |
> | Plumbing Repair: | - *Plumbing fixtures will be tagged out of service upon failure.* |
> | Structural & Paint: | - *Damaged walls, ceilings, floors and door closers will not be repaired except for safety and security.* |

Approximately 100 FTE positions will be eliminated requiring as many as 30 forced layoffs and significant reductions in the number of student employees.

Physical Plant has always responded to the University's budget challenges in the "Can Do" spirit. However, it is obvious that additional cuts of 10% to 20% will cause a degradation of the teaching, research and public service environment approaching the intolerable.

CONTINUED POSITIVE SUPPORT OF THE ACADEMIC MISSION

In accordance with its service priority guidelines, Physical Plant will provide the best environment possible with the dollars available.   DWC/execmm/2/17/93

Custodial Rightsizing: Minimizing the Trauma

Joe Spoonemore

The APPA Rightsizing Survey revealed that 80 percent of those surveyed have experienced some form of budget reduction in the last two years. Annual budget cuts have averaged 3 to 5 percent but many institutions experienced cuts of greater than 10 percent.

At Washington State University we initiated a similar survey of our peer institutions—largely land-grant, graduate-degree awarding, research universities of similar physical size. We unhappily discovered that 70 percent of our peer group had been subjected to budget cuts in the last two years—with some annual cuts in excess of 20 percent! One university experienced a 28 percent cut in a single year, while another was cut 27 percent over the last two years. Even a carry-forward budget, which would seem almost palatable, is effectively a 3 to 5 percent cut when inflation is accounted for. At least among the peers surveyed, no one is optimistic that the austere budget climate is likely to change significantly in the foreseeable future.

Furthermore, facilities organizations are disproportionately affected by budget reductions relative to their peer departments on campus. A university-wide reduction of 5 percent commonly translates into a 10 percent cut at the facilities level.

An interesting statistic can be found in the National Association of College and University Business Officers (NACUBO) publication *Practical Approaches to Rightsizing*. The publication references the U.S. Equal Employment Opportunity Commission study that found that while the number of service maintenance staff at colleges and universities during the period of 1975-90 had declined by 1.9 percent, the faculty had in fact increased by 15.2 percent, administration by 34.3 percent, other professionals by 106.8 percent, clerical by 22.5 percent, and paraprofessional by 30.3 percent (p. viii). It would appear that the facilities service function is viewed as expendable.

While facilities services may be devalued within the institution, however, to the public at large, as supported by a study by the Carnegie Foundation for the Advancement of Teaching,[1] the number one factor in choosing a college is the campus visit. When prospective students were questioned as to the most influential factor considered during the campus visit, 62 percent said "appearance of the grounds and buildings." Thus, the practice of reducing facilities staffing levels places at risk the institution's ability to attract prospective students, parents, faculty, staff, and benefactors. The expectations of the campus community do not change in concert with the decline in facilities staff. Yet facilities departments are expected to maintain service levels and system reliability and limit additions to the disquieting list of deferred maintenance items. In the survey of WSU peer institutions we discovered that the very program that most directly affects both deferred maintenance and system reliability, preventive maintenance, has been reduced on the average by 50 percent. Of the twenty-seven peer institutions, ten state that their PM efficiency has dropped below 30 percent!

The bottom line is that fiscal austerity is a fact of life for the foreseeable future. It has had a severe and potentially irreversible impact on our ability to satisfy our mission and we can expect to be continually challenged to "rightsize" our organizations.

The Custodial Element

Unique among the divisions typically under the direction of the facilities officer is the custodial department. It typically

- Has the greatest number of individuals in an "entry level" classifications.
- Has the highest level of turnover.
- Requires the most well-defined training program.
- Offers the greatest opportunity to consistently interact with the customer and thereby affect physical plant public relations.
- Inordinately challenges the supervisory and interpersonal skills of the leads and supervisors.
- Commands the lowest salary.
- Is the least complicated in terms of task assignment and effort verification.
- Has the highest impact (along with the grounds department) on the level of campus attractiveness.
- Is most often subjected to "contracting out" pressure.

Unlike the insidious infrastructure erosion that follows the decline of routine planned maintenance, custodial effort deviation is almost immediately detectable. Customers react to reduced service levels as soon as the morning after, when they call to report that the custodian failed to empty the waste basket. On the other hand, the university community is quite oblivious to steady declines in infrastructure integrity and system reliability that will ultimately result in traumatic failure. The dynamics of custodial service are therefore more easily studied, compared, and tested.

"Contracting Out" Custodial Services

As noted in the previous list of unique custodial characteristics, one of the recurring suggestions regarding custodial rightsizing is to simply contract it out. This sounds like an inviting concept to the uninitiated. A survey by *Cleaning Management* magazine (April 1994) found that 4.4 percent of the colleges and universities now contracting out custodial work had used in-house forces in the past five years. However, they also discovered that an identical percentage, 4.4 percent, moved back to in-house forces after having experienced cleaning by contractor. The most graphic movement was in the hospital arena, where 10.3 percent of formerly contracted facilities opted for in-house cleaning. Movement toward contracting in hospitals, by comparison, was only 1.2 percent.

Not wishing to leave a rightsizing stone unturned, the WSU custodial department prepared a comprehensive survey with the intent of analyzing the touted benefits of contracted custodial services. We were especially interested in those institutions that had both contract and in-house services. What we discovered, quite frankly, was a serious lack of understanding of the detailed cost and capabilities of either contract *or* in-house service.

"Contract" advocates frequently recited the litany of the custodial contractors, who state that

- You will enjoy economies of scale in that we offer region-wide buying power and an employee recruiting pool of specialized labor.
- We can do a better job because we are more current on products, equipment, and processes.
- You can leave the cleaning to us while you concentrate on other areas reporting to you.

"In-house" advocates frequently referred to the advantages of owner provided custodial forces as they relate to

- The positive maintenance of morale.
- The use of in-house custodial ranks as an entry-level for potential promotion to other in-house maintenance/construction craft positions.
- Limited staff turnover (contract rebids can result in wholesale turnover of supervision and staff).
- Higher security level.
- Higher level of training.
- The greater sensitivity of in-house staff to external economies such as energy conservation.
- Greater level of customer rapport.
- Limited need to maintain in-house supervisory staff to monitor the performance of contract personnel.

- Greater sense of ownership, motivation, dedication, and loyalty.
- Greater staff involvement in departmental decision-making.

What we discovered in our survey was that no matter which option is chosen, you *get what you pay for.* Herein lies another conundrum—*exactly* what services are you getting? And, what *exactly* is it costing you? In answer to the first question, we found that, in addition to classical responsibilities, the in-house forces typically change lights, lock and unlock, provide 24-hour call-back service, do special projects and set-ups, refinish hardwoods, and pursue significant technical training. The contract services frequently will not perform any of these additional services without an additional charge. The contract supervisor-to-custodian ratio is one supervisor for anywhere from ten to twenty-three custodians. The number of in-house supervisors dedicated to monitoring the contractor varies from one per sixteen, to one per fifty-three. (Curiously, one to sixteen was the average for *in-house* supervisors who managed *in-house* staff.) IBM recommends a target ratio of one supervisor for fifteen staff, with a minimum of one to ten.

Also, the contractors tend to assume the graveyard shift, whereas in-house forces are more evenly split between day and swing shifts. The lesson to be learned here is that almost a one-to-one ratio of in-house supervisor to contract supervisor is required to manage and monitor the contract staff. This cost is frequently ignored in cost-per-square-foot calculations.

Addressing the cost question is admittedly something of a challenge. Based on assumed overhead cost and the measures of the area actually cleaned, we found costs per square foot for in-house forces to vary from $0.60 per square foot to a high of $2.26 per square foot in an institution using contract management of in-house forces. Contract cleaning costs varied from a high of $0.85 per square foot to a low of $0.26 per square foot Again, you get what you pay for. *Cleaning Management* magazine notes a national average cost of $0.96 per square foot for colleges and universities, which is significantly lower than that for all other facility types, such as K-12 at $1.32, private office buildings at $1.42, and hospitals at $2.47. The $0.26 figure is generated by establishing an astounding contract staff assignment ratio of 78,500 square feet per person. The *Cleaning Management* survey found the average for colleges and universities to be 23,900 square feet per FTE. As one might expect, service frequencies are severely reduced in the $0.26 per square foot case—for example, by giving restrooms attention only *three times per week*. In addition, staff is paid only $5.00 per hour.

Should the facilities department decide to engage a custodial contractor (a decision which has been made by 2.4 percent of colleges and universities with enrollment over 20,000[2]), the following suggestions are offered by those currently contracting. Insist on

- Theft and damage bonding.
- A competitive wage schedule.
- Certified payroll with a predetermined minimum quantity of worker hours prior to monthly payment.
- Formal certifiable training.
- A carefully and comprehensively written specification with provisions for termination of unsatisfactory bidder, inflation factors, renewal options, and prices for every conceivable "special service."
- Attracting several capable bidders.
- Involving more than one contractor if possible.
- Very close monitoring of contractor performance with provisions for payment deductions for failure to perform and/or performance bonuses.

A novel approach to contracting is to contract with individual workers for custodial service. In one institution this worked well until the faculty became involved and insisted that the contractors should be given fringe benefits equal to the in-house staff. Once annual leave, sick leave, and generous health insurance packages were added, the cost effectiveness of the contract agreements disappeared.

Be aware that a contractor will first determine your cost of service and then will offer a lower figure, which will usually apply only for the first year. The common practice is to request the use of your equipment, to invest nothing in the maintenance of custodial facilities, and to assess an additional charge for every little service that is not specifically spelled out in the contract. Once in-house staff is dispersed and the equipment is timed-out, your options are limited. At this point, contract prices tend to rise. One institution in the study reported that even though their contract custodial costs currently exceed their projected in-house costs, they cannot afford the start-up costs to renew an in-house service.

Under some circumstances, however, contracting appears to work well. Your ace in the hole is to carefully review the contracting option with other institutions in your area that are currently outsourcing their custodial work. Having carefully reviewed the attractive aspects of contract custodial services, and knowing that any attempt to contract out was a clear violation of state law, the decision was made to make our in-house staff as productive and competitive as possible. A brief review of our experience in rightsizing our in-house custodial division follows.

Rightsizing In-House Services at Washington State

Before one begins the task of attempting to rightsize the in-house custodial staff, some basic questions must be answered. Have you considered the mission of the university and of the physical plant? Does your custodial staff buy into the mission? Do they even know what it is? At Washington State, these questions were agenda items for our periodic group meetings between physical plant management and custodial building groups. Having reiterated the collective sense of our mission in annual all-physical-plant meetings and also in our newsletter, you can imagine our chagrin when one of our custodians stepped forward and announced that the mission of the university was to promote peace, prevent hunger, and stop environmental degradation. Following this slightly-off-the-mark comment, the group began to zero in on the mission of the university, which we ultimately decided was liberally paraphrased as:

> In keeping with the traditions and responsibilities of its land-grant status, the mission of the university is to provide instruction, research, and public service in the liberal arts, pure sciences,

*agriculture, home economics, business, health sciences, veteri-
nary medicine, and engineering. In concert with this mandate the
university will develop responsible citizens, broaden the intellectual scope of its students, provide professional/technical skills
needed by society, and promote intellectual curiosity, integrity,
responsibility, and moral values.*

We then turned our attention to the development of the
mission of the custodial department. What we arrived at was
that they were "responsible for the cost-effective provision of a
safe, healthful, pleasing environment that is conducive to the
preservation of our facilities and promotes the education,
research, and extension mission of the university."

With our mission firmly in mind then, we proceeded with the
rightsizing process. First, we reviewed the expectations of the
administration and key members of the campus community.
Using the APPA *Custodial Staffing Guidelines* (1992), we determined that we would target Level 3—Casual Inattention. Some
administrative individuals, of course, held out for Level 1
service on a Level 5 budget—good trick if you can pull it off. It
was generally felt, ultimately, that we could satisfy the mission
of the university and weather a 16.5 percent budget cut over
the 1992-94 period, at least in the short-term, with a Level 3
effort.

Custodial Assignment Ratio

Unlike other inter-university statistics, the staffing ratio for
custodians on a gross-square-feet-per-FTE basis is fairly
straightforward and easily understood by even the most uninitiated. To better illustrate what these numbers mean, one can
simply divide the assigned cleaning area by the square footage
of an average home (1,500 square feet). A cleaning ratio of
30,000 square feet is the equivalent of cleaning twenty homes
every work day! This comparison usually opens some eyes. It
is fairly easy to calculate the gross area covered and divide it
by your custodial FTE.

A survey of the twenty-two peer institutions in July 1993
revealed an assignment ratio from 15,000 to 60,000 per FTE,
with an average of 30,500 on a gross-square-foot basis. Washington State University ranked second from the bottom, with
47,000 gross square feet per custodian. A ratio of 60,000:1 is
almost incomprehensible, but must be well into Level 5—Un-
kempt Neglect. Little comfort can be found in the peer average

of 30,500, because it places the entire peer group approximately in the middle of Level 3 and well below (in terms of service) the previously stated national average of 23,000.

At WSU, our 47,000 gross square foot figure translates to 33,200 cleanable square feet (CSU), which is defined as the inside area of the room as measured from wall-to-wall. How, then, were we to aspire to Level 3 service?

Maximizing the Opportunity

Most organizations or systems can periodically take advantage of the theory of continuous improvement or "tweaking." Our custodial operation was no exception. We did have and continue to enjoy a major advantage, however, in that we are blessed with a stable, dedicated, and motivated staff. When introduced to the problem of successive cuts of 6.5 and 10 percent, the collective can-do response was, "O.K., what can we do to minimize the trauma to the department and our customers and maximize our mission effectiveness?"

Initially, a proposal was prepared to extend our general service frequencies (see detail of current frequencies—Table 1). Exemplary of our service realignment are the frequency changes made in our private offices which are as follows:

	Before	After
Dust Mop	3 x week	2 x week
Vacuum	3 x week	1 x week
Empty Trash	Daily	2 x week
Dust/Clean Phones	2 x week	1 x month
Spot Mop	2 x week	As needed
Windows	Annually	1 x 7 years

Following endorsement by the administration, the proposal was taken to the deans in concert with their chairs. With their unanimous support, the changes were publicized and effected.

The service frequency shift alone could not have won the day without the following intra-physical plant initiatives:

- Improvement in quality, sophistication, and accessibility of equipment.
- Offering 9-month appointments and three-fourths time positions.

Table 1
General custodial service frequencies, Washington State University
physical plant, July 1993.

Area/Task   Frequency

Restrooms and Locker Rooms
  sweep and mop floors   daily
  empty trash   daily
  disinfect surfaces   daily
  deep clean fixtures   1 x week
  dust ventilation fixtures   1 x week

Hallways, Entries, and Main stairs:
  sweep floors   daily
  spot clean entry galss   daily
  remove trash   daily
  clean fountains   daily
  spot mop floors   daily
  mop or auto scrub   as needed
  vacuum entry mats   as needed
  dust   as needed

Stairs—secondary
  sweep   1 x week
  remove trash   daily
  spot mop   as needed
  dust   1 x month
  mop entire stairs   as needed

Classrooms:
  pick up floor litter   daily
  empty trash   daily
  straighten chairs   daily
  spot mop floors   daily
  clean chalkboard with felt eraser   daily
  clean chalk tray and restock chalk   daily

clean chalkboard with
  custodian eraser   1 x week
sweep or vacuum floor   2 x week
dust air ventilation fixtures   1 x month
mop entire floor   as needed

Labs:
sweep floors   2 x week
empty trash   2 x week
spot mop floors   as needed
mop entire floor   as needed

Shops:
sweep floors   2 x week
empty trash   2 x week
spot mop floors   as needed
mop entire floors   as needed

Reception Area:
sweep or vacuum floors   2 x week
empty trash   3 x week
mop floor   1 x week
dust   1 x month

Main Offices:
sweep floors   2 x week
vacuum floors   1 x week
empty trash   2 x week
dust   1 x month
spot mop   as needed

Private Offices:
sweep floors   2 x week
vacuum floors   1 x week
empty trash   2 x week
dust   1 x month
spot mop   as needed

- Emphasis on formal, regimented training of new employees.
- Division of workforce into two shifts. Day shift is from 5:00 a.m. to 1:30 p.m. The swing shift is from 5:00 p.m. until 1:30 a.m.
- Reduction in force by 10 percent, largely by elimination of unfilled custodial positions and one supervisor position.
- Insist that trades do more picking up after themselves.
- Review of vending and recycling activities with respect to potential for subsidizing attendant custodial effort.
- Elimination of toilet seat covers.
- Continue use of rolled paper towels rather than cloth or folded paper.
- Transfer of sanitary napkin dispensers to vending services and limiting installations to centralized facilities.
- Request that if waste baskets fill prematurely they be placed in the hallway.
- Make cleaning materials available to occupants should they choose to supplement our efforts.
- Request that instructors assist us in policing the use of food and drink in classrooms.
- Resumption of reporting letters of commendation in the Physical Plant newsletter.
- Emphasize the practice of presenting congratulatory letters to individuals with perfect attendance records of six months or more.
- Curtail practice of hiring students for "time-slip" service. Students are cost effective only if you don't consider the inordinate supervisory effort required to recruit, train, and direct them. Not only must they be trained on routine custodial procedures but they must be either inoculated for Hepatitis B or afforded post-inoculation and schooled on MSDS. This is no small or cost-free task when the high rate of turnover is considered.
- Offer summer craft positions to qualified custodians thereby fulfilling the need for temporary craftspersons while appropriately reducing summertime custodial staff. This process has been taken to a much higher level by

Indiana University and Purdue University, who have transferred fourteen and ten custodians respectively to trades areas for the summer construction period.[3]

How Are We Doing?

To date, we have had nothing but total cooperation and support from the campus customers. Our frequency of written commendations has not diminished, and the custodians continue to receive the vast majority of all physical plant kudos. The change from a largely swing/graveyard structure to a 54 percent day/46 percent swing format has succeeded far beyond our expectations. We have been pleased to note an enhanced custodial/customer relationship, to the point where the customer frequently becomes adamantly opposed to proposed custodial transfers. We have not suffered the expected gross reduction in efficiency, partly because the 5:00 a.m. start allows sufficient time to address high-traffic areas. The new shift structure also allows the day shift to do the unlocking and service the most difficult areas prior to the arrival of the occupants. A maximum amount of facility security is provided with the exception of a three-and-a-half-hour hiatus between 1:30 a.m. and 5:00 a.m. Finally, we were amazed that all of our day shift positions were filled by voluntary transfer. This fortuitously met the desires of both the administration and the staff—a formula that is all too frequently difficult to satisfy.

Can we survive another round of budget cutting? Surely, but as we move inexorably toward Level 5 we will see serious morale declines in both the physical plant ranks as well as in the faculty and staff circles. With the associated deterioration of our facilities, can we rely on increased capital support for deferred maintenance? Probably not.

If nothing else, I believe that we have shown that it is possible to continue to function with an exaggerated assignment ratio of one FTE per 47,000 gross square feet and still fulfill our mission, at least at a Service Level 3. I am not optimistic that a repeat of this process will be successful by any standard should we face yet another budget reduction.

"Downsizing" vs. "Dumbsizing"

We read it in the newspapers and journals and we are assaulted by it in the evening news. Layoffs, the end result of dramatic downsizing, seem to be in vogue in corporate America. The numbers are staggering: Xerox -10,000; Kodak - 12,000; Philip Morris - 14,000; Boeing - 28,000; IBM - 35,000; and the leader of the pack, Sears, with an astounding 50,000 layoffs.[4]

According to one source, "As of September 1993, 514 companies in the United States had disclosed plans to eliminate another 450,000 positions."[5]

Where are we going? Is this really the correct reaction to our loss of competitive prowess? Numerous economists disagree. They believe that we should be looking for ways to increase productivity and creativity, thereby utilizing the tremendous investment in personnel and preserving the incalculable value of ownership and company loyalty. These traits are simply not available through outsourcing or the constant threats of layoffs.

The facts are that the results of downsizing are largely negative, according to some research. "In 1992, the American Management Association conducted a survey of some 500 companies that had gone through downsizing since 1987. More than 75 percent reported a collapse of employee morale. Two-thirds could see no increase in efficiency, and less than one-half had any improvement in profits."[6]

Are the survivors obliged to work harder? You bet they are! Kim Cameron at the University of Michigan studied white-collar downsizing in the auto industry between 1986 and 1990. He found that these workers were forced to increase their work hours by 30 percent to meet expectations. Bernard Baumohl noted that as of February 1993 "the manufacturing workweek stretched to 41.5 hours, the longest in 27 years."[7]

In addition to the obvious danger of increased stress and discontent and declining loyalty and creativity, a downsizing organization also runs the risk of increased union activity. This is exactly what happened at Washington State. Following an ill-advised threat by a key administrator that most of the custodial responsibilities would be outsourced, the union, which previously held a partnership role, began filing a fusillade of grievances, initiated a serious membership drive, and began forming a new bargaining unit.

Even though facilities managers walk the tightrope between accomplishing their mission and meeting the budgetary expectations of the administration, it appears that we can still minimize the trauma and maximize the opportunity. At WSU, although we have reduced our custodial staffing level, we have successfully avoided a catastrophic decline in service and facility quality by incorporating a team effort. The team includes our customers, physical plant management, university administration, and, most important, our custodial staff. Custodial morale is above average, grievances have never been lower, and the level of rapport with our customers has been sustained.

Notes

1. *Change.* January/February 1986.

2. "The Make-or-Buy Decision: The Organization of U.S. Campus Plant Operations." Malcolm Getz, Jon M. Gullette, Diane E. Kilpatrick, and John J. Siegfried. *Facilities Manager,* Spring 1994.

3. Davis and Huffard, *Proceedings of the 1993 Annual Meeting,* APPA, 1993.

4. *Time,* April 28, 1994.

5. Rakstis, Ted J. *Kiwanis.* April 1994.

6. Ibid.

7. Baumohl, Bernard. *Time,* March 15, 1993.

The Human Element

Pieter J. van der Have

The American Management Association reveals that the number of companies trimming their workforces continues to rise. A recent survey found that the percentage of such firms has risen from 46.1 percent in 1992 to 46.6 percent in 1993. Following a similar trend, the percentage of the workforce being reduced has also grown, from 9.3 percent in 1992 to 10.4 percent in 1993. Most affected, incidentally, were hourly employees (47 percent), followed by professional and technical employees (20 percent), middle managers (19 percent), and supervisors (15 percent).

In the private sector, organizations have moved toward the creation of slim and trim command centers where corporate staff have been drastically reduced and levels of management deemed unnecessary have been eliminated. Regardless of which level of staff is affected, there are common elements to the process.

Adjusting staffing levels as a strategic element of rightsizing may be accomplished through several processes, three of which are across-the-board cuts, voluntary retirement, or surgical reductions. Some managers may choose to use a hybrid of approaches. Any one of these options, unless it is carefully thought through, may lead to serious and uncontrolled degradation in service levels. The purpose of this chapter is to help managers to think through the turmoil of staff reduction with the purpose of helping assure the long-term health of the organization.

Some employers tend to forget the sizable investment they have made in their people—frequently as much or more as they have in their capital assets. As a result, long-term financial commitments may linger long after the employee is gone. Large organizations in the private sector, such as General Motors, IBM, and notable others, find these long-lasting obligations especially expensive and cumbersome to incorporate into their new strategic plans. They find themselves in a quagmire of personnel expense that seems to be self-perpetuating.

Rightsizing as an organizational response requires the creation of a culture that emphasizes a value-based work environment. Traditional work values, such as trust and caring, need to be emphasized in order to maintain a reasonable amount of loyalty to the organization. The way many of us deal with the human elements of rightsizing appears antithetical to trust and caring. In this shaky environment, we often forget we have two groups of individuals with whom we have to relate: those who are (about to be) laid off and those who are not (yet).

Managers in the United States have, in isolated cases, shown sensitivity to the staff about to be laid off. Unfortunately, that level of sensitivity is significantly less than that demonstrated in other parts of the world. We traditionally place a fairly low emphasis on retraining staff to help them cope with being unemployed and to help them find other employment.

Employers in the United States have been less concerned about the plight of the disadvantaged, who are more likely to consist of low-income individuals with little work experience, an unstable work history, and low skill levels. Thus, whether they are to be cut loose or retained, they are likely to be considered expendable. Some authors suggest that other, "outsider" groups are also likely to suffer more than the (locally) dominant group. This outsider status may be based on gender, race, religion, sexual orientation, or other characteristics. If management decides to eliminate certain job classifications where the incumbents tend to fall in a certain ethnic (or other minority classification) category, management will have to demonstrate tremendous sensitivity in working with and counseling those individuals. The National Labor Relations Act, the

Labor Management Relations Act, the Fair Labor Standards Act, Title VII of the Civil Rights Act of 1964, the Age Discrimination in Employment Act, and now the Americans with Disabilities Act are among the federal laws of which management has to be cognizant. There are probably also a number of state or local statutes that may apply.

The Herman Miller, Steelcase, and Boeing corporations have been pioneers in demonstrating a more humane approach to rightsizing. Organizations are now beginning to more often consider the needs of staff who are soon to be laid off. They are using such techniques as

- Providing advance notice.
- Counseling (occasionally with significant others).
- Special training in job-finding skills.
- Voluntary transfers to help individuals who are to fall victim to rightsizing cope, adjust, survive, and, on occasion, improve themselves.

As was said at the beginning of this chapter, there is another group of employees with whom we have to concern ourselves—those who escape the layoffs. They are the lucky ones. Or are they?

As the interested reader reviews the literature regarding rightsizing, one fact becomes evident: many organizations about to undertake the journey toward rightsizing consistently forgot or ignored the people on whom they were going to rely to make their companies rebound after the staff reductions. They failed to consider the basic needs of those who remain behind. They failed to recognize people issues. Management always assumed survivors would be grateful and unfailingly loyal. After all, they were allowed to keep their jobs. What else could they possibly want? Survivors in general have never received the same level of attention as those whose positions are cut. Certain experts are now openly suggesting this as one of the primary reasons for the unsatisfactory results often seen after rightsizing efforts.

Research now indicates that those who are not terminated are often extremely uncomfortable with their roles in the new structure. As one might anticipate, the result can often be a disproportionate decrease in output and productivity, keeping the bottom line unsatisfactory and leading management to conclude further rightsizing may be justified. Perhaps ironically, the attitude and morale of the survivors may in part be determined by how the employer prepares those to be laid off for what awaits them. The survivors often gauge the sincerity of corporate leaders by how they perceive management handled recent staff reductions.

There are a few examples of employers who demonstrated the right way to work with the people who were about to be laid off. Boeing is considered one success story. Once its corporate leaders determined a need to rightsize the company, they did not attempt to keep it secret. Eighteen months before the openly communicated "reduction" date, the human resources department started working with employees by holding training sessions, teaching people how to cope, or helping them get into retraining programs. Open discussions were a common forum. Management reviewed with staff its financial and productivity reports to explain its decision, so that when the inevitable time came, impact on morale was relatively minor. Everyone knew and understood. All employees had been invited to participate in the entire process. They were thus familiar with the strategic issues that necessitated rightsizing. Those whose positions were eliminated had many opportunities extended to them to help them move on with their lives and to reduce the extreme rancor that so often accompanies downsizing. Those who were to remain understood and generally accepted the strategic plan mapping out the future.

The leadership of the University of Utah also recognized early on that being fair to all staff was critical to the success of its 1987 rightsizing process. Mostly by instinct, management recognized that morale of both the survivors and the casualties would have a long-term impact on the success and failure of the effort, and on the success of the organization. The University of Utah worked long and hard to help those whose positions were going to be eliminated and to support those who were going to stay on. As a result, all but four out of nearly 100 full-time staff found other employment on campus or in the community before the agreed-upon date. Productivity stayed level, turnover did not increase, and morale, while not exuberant, stayed constant.

Survivors Need Help Too...

Survivors may not always be as grateful for surviving as management might expect. They deal with feelings of anger, guilt, and distrust.

Metaphor of the Surviving Children

Imagine a family: a father, a mother, and four children. The family has been together for a long time, living in a loving, nurturing, trusting environment. The parents take care of the children, who reciprocate by being good.

Every morning, the family sits down to breakfast, a ritual that functions as a bonding experience, somewhat akin to an organizational staff meeting. One morning, the children sense that something is wrong. The parents exchange a few furtive glances, appear nervous, and after painful silence, the mother speaks. "Father and I have reviewed the family budget," she says, looking down at her plate, avoiding eye contact, "and we just don't have enough money to make ends meet!" She forces herself to look around the table and continues, "As much as we would like to, we just can't afford to feed and clothe all four of you." After another silence she points a finger. "You two must go!"

"It's nothing personal," explains the father as he passes out a sheet of paper to each of the children. "As you can see by the numbers in front of you, it's simply an economic decision — we really have no choice." He continues, forcing a smile, "We have arranged for your aunt and uncle to help you get settled, to aid in your transition."

The next morning, the two remaining children are greeted by a table on which only four places have been set. Two chairs have been removed. All physical evidence of the other two children has vanished. The emotional evidence is suppressed and ignored. No one talks about the two who have disappeared. The parents emphasize to the two remaining children, the survivors, that they should be grateful, "since, after all, you've been allowed to remain in the family." To show their gratitude, the remaining children will be expected to work harder on the family chores. The father explains that "the workload remains the same even though there are two less of you." The mother explains that "this will make us a closer family!"

—Noer, David M., *Healing the Wounds*, p. 8

It is only a small stretch to refer to the veterans of the wars, including Vietnam, who manifested survivor sickness. Aleksandr Solzhenitsyn wrote on this type of demoralizing human phenomenon. Elizabeth Kubler-Ross, a noted survivor of the Holocaust, wrote on the subject in her book *On Death and Dying*.

While in the extermination camps, she noted human emotions as they manifested themselves in that horrible environment. She identifies the following stages in the process of "death and dying."

1. Denial

2. Anger, including rage, envy, and resentment

3. Bargaining

4. Depression, which includes sadness, gloominess, pessimism, guilt, and feelings of worthlessness

5. Acceptance (not to be equated with happiness)

Although layoffs are certainly less devastating than death in terms of overall human significance, the stages that she identifies can be applied to a layoff environment, to both the victims and the survivors. Research also suggests it takes longer for survivors to work their way through these five stages than it does the victims. The latter often do find other employment where they once again have an opportunity to develop positive feelings and attitudes. The survivors, on the other hand, are left in the environment that gave rise to these feelings—the environment that, through inaction or insensitivity, allows those feelings to breed, brood, and grow.

People naturally experience stress and generally do not need or want more. For most, 70 percent of the stress is "baggage," which clings like a barnacle. It is caused by events from the past; events over which we no longer have any control. The future and its unknown elements account for a surprising 20 percent of our stress. Only 10 percent is attributable to events in the present.

In the rightsizing scenario, then, by carefully and effectively communicating with the survivors, the management team can help mitigate up to 30 percent of survivors' stress. Employees may feel grateful not to have been terminated, but they may not readily accept other work assignments, reductions in pay, or changes in working hours or location. Even in the most benevolent of organizations, there may well be individuals who will take any and every opportunity to argue, resist, and fight back. There have been cases of sabotage and willful destruction, and worse, physical violence. Witness the experiences of the U.S. Postal Service in the early 1990s.

A survey conducted by Right Associates shows how survivors of rightsizing or downsizing have low levels of self-confidence, show distrust in the organization, suffer from acute work-related stress, and doubt their roles in the new organization. Right Associates recommends guidelines on motivating surviving employees. Conceivably, certain measures can and should be taken well before the actual rightsizing (such as was done at the University of Utah), whether or not it involves a reduction in force. Properly timing termination notices, offering secure access to benefits, and providing training for managers on how to inform and deal with staff are among methods management can use to address the fears and insecurities of even those whose positions will not be eliminated.

As indicated before, trust is the most important element of the rightsizing effort. The issue of job security has become a prime concern to employers and employees alike. Organizations in the private sector as well as in higher education are continuously striving to remain competitive. Unfortunately, this is most often accomplished through continuous downsizing. Employers are more recently beginning to realize employees will lose trust in them if they continue to make empty promises of job security. To improve such shaky relationships, employees and employers need to establish a new understanding that addresses the needs of all parties. One might consider the concept of "continuous human improvement," where employee and employer are both committed to achieving organizational goals through the application of new technology, teamwork, and training and educational programs.

Leaders have to use any and all opportunities to deal with and mitigate unreasonable stress and anxiety created by a rightsizing effort. After layoffs, management should assess the concerns of all remaining staff, and then address those concerns.

Another frequently unrecognized factor is the needs of the managers who have to do the firing. Although they may agree with where the organization is going, they may still see themselves as doing intentional harm to others, something many are not comfortable with. Managers may feel they are acting as assassins, "terminating" or "taking out" their fellow employees. They may have to deal with feelings of having betrayed the trust placed in them by their associates, of being disloyal to them.

In an environment of rightsizing the manager has to evolve into a leader, into a visionary. Each one has to develop the skills to influence the organization's competitive environment, change the organizational culture, and upgrade the skills, abilities, and dedication of the people. This goes beyond the physical structure; this invisible, intangible structure is the aspect of rightsizing the successful leader has to address and deal with if rightsizing is to succeed.

Ironically, managers often dedicate themselves to the physical structure when attempting to rightsize. That is like having a canoe but no paddles: it will not get anywhere! Even IBM and General Motors have found they cannot simply organize around people. Ideas and ideals are the mortar that hold the whole structure together. Sears, for example, may still not have fully formulated what it is all about. Does it yet know what it wants to be? It appears to some analysts that Sears still wants to be successful in the same way it was before. Until recently, Sears did not recognize its competition: K-Mart, and later, Wal-Mart. How then can it generate any kind of corporate loyalty and sense of mission among its staff?

Management has to understand empowerment. Equally important, surviving employees must feel genuinely empowered. They have to focus on essential processes, which they certainly can't do if those processes are not defined in recognizable terms reflective of the organization's vision and strategic plan. The successful manager has to be able identify processes that promote the involvement of front-line workers in team-based processes. For example, to be successful today, a higher education facilities organization must already have standards programs in place. Programs such as planned and preventive maintenance programs, custodial standards, grounds standards, and cost accounting systems with meaningful cost centers have already helped establish an informed environment.

People who perform the work have hands-on knowledge they can use to identify processes that support the expressed mission of the organization. Using this knowledge is essential, both to build a meaningful program and to help the survivors rebuild a sense of dignity and loyalty. It is important to realize that if handled incorrectly, more of the better qualified and motivated staff may choose to go elsewhere. Left behind will be those who have no other place to go.

Historically, in areas where unionization is prevalent, such flexibility might have been unrealistic. In recent years, however, both management and union leaders have begun to realize (albeit both somewhat slowly and reluctantly) that the dignity of all staff is something to be considered and valued. More often now, both groups are accepting flexibility as a way of responding to today's economically based mandates.

The phrase "paradigm shift" is gaining popularity. Managers are both leaders and participants in effecting a paradigm shift within the organization. When successful, these visionary managers can provide meaning to all team members about what will happen to the total organization. If they are unsuccessful, the employees will feel like they are blatantly being asked to do more with less.

A successful paradigm shift will include the following elements:

- Shift from organizational strategies that promote dependence to those that promote independence, or preferably, interdependence.
- Shift from the historically encouraged need for belonging to the necessity for autonomy.
- Shift from the perception of the leader as savior to the leader as helper.
- Shift from the desire for permanence to the reality of change.

Traditional managers have to invest much of themselves in this process, because for many these changes contradict what they had to do to get where they are! Managers not only have to participate in the change, they have to perpetually model— they have to coach.

Institutional leaders, especially human resources managers, have to be aware of the agreements or employment contracts used at their own institutions. When endeavoring to implement rightsizing strategies, the leaders must be aware of all applicable laws and policies as well as the current cultural and socioeconomic climate of the local community. Immediate steps must be taken, including a review of personnel policies, performance evaluation systems, benefit plans, collective bargaining, and employment agreements (whether written or verbal). The training of managers at all levels must receive priority. Finally, leaders must document all steps taken, assessments, and decisions affecting the rightsizing effort. Commitment and communication must be steadfastly maintained. It is critical that all the participants in an organization going through rightsizing be honest, communicate openly, and be fair.

In evaluating options for rightsizing, the effective leader encourages his or her players to be fully sensitive of cause-and-effect relationships and to make provisions accordingly. The facilities professional will continually challenge the way business is done, even when there is no promise or threat of mandated rightsizing efforts. Many of us have used the process of "peer review" to help us identify specific areas that could benefit from rightsizing.

For many of us, rightsizing in an abstract sense may be something we can easily relate to. When it comes, however, to dealing with real-life individuals whose jobs are going to be seriously altered if not eliminated, here are some key processes to keep in mind that can help assure success of the remaining organization.

1. Communicate openly and freely with all players. Do not allow the rumor mill to do your work for you.
2. Be a visionary leader. Make sure you know where *your* organization will go.
3. Develop strategic plans, at all levels within the organization. Include staff from all levels in the discussions.
4. Recognize that you can't determine who is to be laid off by consensus. However, having open discussions involving key individuals is essential.
5. Keep all staff informed of the layoff process. Notify privately where appropriate, but communicate the big picture.
6. Keep benefit options available to terminated staff as long as economically feasible after termination.

7. Develop and maintain trust. Guarantee a trusting relationship among the managers on your team. (If they talk badly about one another or other units in front of their subordinates, the whole organization and every staff member in it will suffer.) Cultivate a comfortable feeling of interdependence among all survivors.

8. The survivors will also suffer from very intense feelings during and after any layoffs. Be willing to work with them on resolving those feelings. Help them to deal with "survivor illness" by making appropriate and safe guarantees about the future. Also, wherever possible provide advanced technology to help them meet higher performance expectations.

9. Managers are not superhuman. Most carry with them feelings of guilt and pain after they have fired someone. Recognize that their trusting relationship with their staff has been compromised. Also realize their trust in senior management (you?) has been shaken. Deal with these phenomena through open communication and active listening. Provide counseling and training to them as well.

10. Provide constant and honest feedback to everyone regarding progress being made toward agreed-upon objectives. Be honest—staff will know when you're faking it before you do.

The real professional plans and does not often have to react. Reactive behavior frequently leads to impulsive creativity. As one APPA member, in offering comments on the Rightsizing Survey, phrased it, "Creativity frequently culminates in short-term efficiency and long-range demise." We can't afford the ignore the details of our real assets: our people.

Conclusion

More than any time in history, mankind faces a crossroads. One path leads to despair and utter hopelessness, the other to total extinction. Let us pray that we have the wisdom to choose correctly.

—Woody Allen

It is easy to allow ourselves to look at this process with a great deal of skepticism. Yet, for most of us in this profession, the primary motivation for doing what we do is the desire to keep our campus a great place for its users while supporting the mission of the institution and assuring the longevity of its investments. We are proud of our institution's physical assets. We gloat unabashedly when visiting peers tell us that our campus is beautiful and one of the best maintained. We admire them for their obvious intelligence and good taste, even though we know deep down we have many significant problems which just are not readily visible. We proudly tell our administrators about the Carnegie Foundation study that revealed that 60 percent of prospective students (and faculty and staff) base their choice of institutions purely on the way the campus looks. As facilities managers, we put in long hours to achieve perfection, even when we know deep down we can never get there.

Rightsizing has been with us forever. Usually it is perceived as downsizing, although that does not necessarily have to be the case. Restructuring, one version of rightsizing, offers opportunities to become more effective at what we are doing, possibly by doing less of it, but doing it better. It means going beyond doing things right, to doing the RIGHT things RIGHT. With careful consideration of the human element, we can achieve that by eliminating those processes, functions, and organizational units (regardless of perceived importance) that do not contribute to the long-term well being of the organization, as defined through the strategic planning process. All that is required is good professional sense, good leadership skills and tools, a willingness to involve our staff members in the planning processes, an ability to build teams and to coach, an unbiased perspective of the welfare of the holistic unit, and a deep-felt pride in the institution and our role within it.

References

Anfuso, D. "Recruitment by the Numbers." *Personnel Journal*, vol.72, no. 12, December 1993.

Clark, C.V. "Downsizing Trounces Diversity." *Black Enterprise*, vol. 24, no. 7, February 1994.

Cross, M. ed. *Managing Workforce Reduction.* New York: Praeger, 1985.

Deal, T.E., and Jenkins, W.A. *Business Officer,* March 1994.

Eisen, R., "Devising a Layoff Contingency Plan." *HR Magazine*, vol. 38, no. 6, June 1993.

Fagiano, D., "The Downside of Downsizing." *Security Management,* vol. 36, no. 10, October 1992.

Hammer, M., and Champy, J. *Reengineering the Corporation: A Manifesto for Business Revolution.* New York: Harper Business, 1993.

Heenan, D.O. "The Right Way to Downsize." *Journal of Business Strategy,* vol. 12, no. 5, September/October 1991.

Hendricks, C. F. *The Rightsizing Remedy.* Homewood, Illinois: Society for Human Resource Management and Business One Irwin, 1992.

Henkoff, R. "Getting Beyond Downsizing." *Fortune,* vol. 129, no. 1, January 10, 1994.

"HR Paints a Bleak Portrait of Downsizing Survivors." *HR Focus,* vol. 70, no. 5, May 1993.

Lawrence, A.T., and Mittman, B.S. "Downsizing on the Upswing." *Personnel,* vol. 68, no. 2, February 1991.

Lively, K. "State Colleges Grapple with Tough Decisions on How to 'Downsize.'" *Chronicle of Higher Education,* vol. 39, no. 22, February 3, 1993.

Loomis, C. J. "Dinosaurs." *Fortune,* May 3, 1993.

Major, M. "Candor Helps Boeing Handle Massive Layoffs." *Public Relations Journal,* vol. 49, no. 12, December 1993.

"More Cuts...Deeper Cuts." *HR Focus,* vol. 70, no. 11, November 1993.

Noer, D. M. *Healing the Wounds.* San Francisco: Jossey-Bass, 1993.

Porter, T.J., and Kenoe, J.G. "Using Activity-Based Costing." *National Productivity Review,* vol. 13, no. 1, Winter 1993.

Seymour, J. "Misapprehending Opportunity as Peril." *PC Week,* vol. 10, no. 46, November 22, 1993.

Seinbach, B. "Continuous Human Improvement." *Training,* vol. 30, no. 10, October 1993.

Siebert, B. "Downsizing: An Overview of Legal Considerations." *Labor Law Journal,* vol. 34, no. 8, August 1992.

Theimer, C.H.R., "How Can I Recharge My Worn-out Staff." *Executive Female,* vol. 17, no. 1, January/February 1994.

Thompson, C.M. "Reorientation Eases the Pain and Loss of Downsizing." *HR Focus,* vol. 69, no. 1, January 1992.

Vasilash, G.S. "The Physics of Government." *Production,* vol. 105, no. 11, November 1993.

Strategic Planning in the Physical Plant Department

Frederick L. Klee

In the good old days now past, colleges and universities grew rapidly to accommodate an increasing number of students. Commensurate with this growth was sufficient money for the construction and maintenance of these new buildings. In recent years, however, the demographics have changed, as have our institutions' ability to fund all of the perceived needs. These changes have had a profound effect on the way we do business. The budgeting process has become competitive; as a result, the plant department now competes with academic programs for funds.

For the most part, this increased competition has had a positive impact on the institutions we serve, but it has also brought serious challenges to facilities operations, since less money is available. It has forced us to critically evaluate projects, to sharpen our presentations to boards and presidents, and to increase the amount of support documentation needed before we move forward on a project.

In that light, it is important for us to move from short-range, yearly budgeting practices to long-range, strategic plans that take into account the objectives of the institution.

A Definition Of Strategic Planning

Approximately 166 of the 388 respondents (approximately 42 percent) to the rightsizing survey indicated that they had already developed strategic plans for their respective facilities management organizations. In telephone interviews, however, it became apparent that in most cases the plan indicated was in fact some portion of the institutional strategic plan that encompassed the physical plant only marginally. In other cases, the plan referred to was actually a master plan for the institution. Indeed, a master plan is only one important part of an overall strategic plan.

A strategic plan organizes the functions of the facilities department according to their importance to the institution as a whole. A well-organized plan starts with the practices that need to be improved or that must be performed to meet the mission of the institution. To accurately assess these functions, the financial and human needs that reflect the future of the operation must first be identified. These functional assessments then provide the institution's leadership with the information they need to make future decisions regarding the institutional infrastructure.

Strategic planning differs from long-range planning in that it tries to identify and resolve issues. Strategic plans are applicable to all organizations, for-profit and nonprofit alike. Long-range plans set in place a process for dealing with the questions raised by the strategic plan. Strategic planning questions include:

1. Where are we going?
2. How do we get there?
3. What is our blueprint for action?
4. How do we know if we are on track?

Without answering these basic questions we cannot set a course for our future that will provide the consistency we need to meet our long-term objectives.

Relating these four questions to the various components of a plan, we can say that "where are we going?" equates to the mission of the organization, and "how do we get there?" relates directly to the strategies we establish to reach our goals. "How do we know if we are on track" can be answered through clearly established, viable measurement criteria that can be used to gather benchmarking data and comparisons, and the question "what is our means to get there?" considers the financial support and control we have.

Reasons for Strategic Planning

Why should we commit to strategic planning? The more significant reasons for doing it are

- It is indispensable to top management's ability to effectively discharge its responsibility.
- It forces managers to ask and answer questions that are of the highest importance to the facilities operation and the institution.
- Planning simulates the future on paper. Not only is it cheaper, but it allows the department to make better decisions now that will affect the future.
- Planning helps top management identify key issues and establish priorities.
- Strategic planning is an excellent way to improve communication and allow everyone to contribute to the decision-making process.
- After completing the exercise, most managers and departments have a better perspective of the institution's responsibilities.

Most institutions have reduced budgets mainly by arbitrarily cutting the dollars available to specific administrative departments. The facilities department, because it is highly visible and generally has the second largest budget after faculty and staff salaries, is traditionally a prime target for reductions. Most often, these reductions are not part of a strategic plan. This haphazard approach explains why the problem of deferred maintenance has mushroomed. It is easier to curtail projects that will affect the future rather than reduce service for current operations because it is our successors who will have to deal with our shortsightedness.

operations because it is our successors who will have to deal with our shortsightedness.

Working through the development of a strategic plan can benefit the facilities department in many ways because it can help the organization to think strategically. By clarifying the future direction of the unit, the plan helps establish priorities, ensures that decisions are made in light of their future consequences, provides a defensible basis for decisions, and allows an organization to exercise maximum discretion in the areas under its control. Strategic planning has been defined as a disciplined effort to produce fundamental decisions and actions that shape and guide what an organization is, what it does, and why it does it.

A strategic plan also helps coordinate decision-making across operating units at an institution. Concentrating on plan development forces the department to focus on the overall strategies of the institution. Such a plan can also improve motivation and morale for the supervisors and others. People in most organizations, at all levels, are interested in participating in the decision-making process, contributing their knowledge to the organization, and finding opportunities to be creative.

Most operations review their comprehensive strategic plans every several years. In the interim years, the department or institution can focus on the subsets of the strategies listed in the plan and resolve a few key issues.

To be effective, the facilities strategic plan must be integrated with that of the institution. The facilities mission must be clearly articulated in terms of support for the institutional mission.

Developing the Strategic Plan

The first step to beginning the strategic planning process is a commitment to the process by the leadership. Other milestones include:

1. Conducting an institutional assessment.
2. Developing a departmental mission statement.
3. Developing departmental vision.
4. Setting departmental strategic goals.

5. Evaluating strengths, weaknesses, opportunities, and threats (SWOT analysis).

A strategic plan should in the end maintain and support the strengths, reduce identified weaknesses, combat all threats, and take advantage of all of the opportunities.

The first step in the strategic planning process then, is to assess the function of the facilities department. We should ask ourselves what we as facilities managers should be doing for our college or university. In general, our responsibilities are to

- Improve the quality of campus life by improving the residence halls and any other spaces used outside of the academic area of the college.
- Support the instructional program by improving classrooms, laboratories, and offices.
- Preserve the asset value of the buildings, grounds, and infrastructure of the institution.
- Contain costs by instituting policies and practices that will reduce future operating expenditures while conserving valuable capital.
- Initiate safety and environmental practices that will reduce the exposure of the institution from external and internal liabilities.

The appropriateness of these goals as basic guidelines for facilities operations can be evaluated as the strategic plan develops.

Building the Planning Team

Commitment to developing the plan generally comes from the leader of the department. That person initiating the process and provides some of the direction he or she sees for the department.

The next task is to identify which persons should be involved in the strategic planning process. In a facilities operation, all of the key supervisors are major players in the development of a plan. These are the people who directly translate the policies and decisions into operational directives. Also important are representatives of the various trade units within the department. These employees are the direct customer contacts who also have a keen sense of the needs of the stakeholders of the department. Like the supervisors, they too are responsible for making decisions on a daily basis. Obtaining the cooperation and commitment of the entire department for a strategic plan requires that these segments are fully involved in its development.

It is important to have a clear agenda for the team that is to assemble and develop the strategic plan. The agenda should include some discussion of the purpose, nature, and process for creating the strategic plan. Some time should also be spent reviewing the experiences that other departments or institutions may have faced in the development of a strategic plan. The review team in the facilities department should become familiar with the elements of the institutional mission statement to ensure correct alignment of the facilities plan.

After the essential members of the group are brought together, some agreement should be formulated that will outline the anticipated outcomes of the planning process. All members must be fully committed to the project. It may be helpful for the team to examine the consequences of not moving ahead with the planning process. The team should also evaluate who will be part of the process, how the process will work, what steps must be taken to reach the goal, and what the timetable will be.

At each of the milestones listed on page 120 the session should conclude with agreement on what the next step will be in the process of developing the plan or if the process should be halted. This review will provide the support the group needs to maintain its commitment to the process.

An Institutional Assessment

It may be important for the team to review and refine a profile of the institution and the department to reinforce the notion of who they are. The following elements might be included:

- Type of institution
- Enrollment, boundaries, equivalent full-time enrollment
- Annual budget for institution and department
- Full-time staff for institution and department

- A list of contracted services
- Renovation projects and schedule of each
- A list of the institution's and department's customers

At the end of these sessions it should be apparent to the team that there is a need for planning for the future. In the next step, the group engages in visioning exercises to develop a mission statement for the department or the sub-unit.

The Mission Statement

The department's mission statement should provide consistency and clarity for all members of the department. This mission statement will be the focus for all planning decisions. To be effective, the statement should have the support of all the team members and it should define the role of the department in terms of the institution in order to gain the support of all stakeholders. A careful and thoughtful review of the institutional mission statement should begin the process.

An institutional mission statement will include some of the following sentiments:

Enable students to become independent, responsible, and thoughtful individuals through a program of education.

To empower the students through a program that awakens the intellect, moral sensitivity, and challenges those students to improve society.

The faculty as the cornerstone of any academic program are dedicated to teaching and setting high standards for students and themselves. The mission of the college is to enable students to become independent, responsible, and thoughtful individuals through a program of liberal education. That education prepares them to live creatively and usefully and to provide leadership for their society in an interdependent world.

The mission for the facilities department may be something a simple as:

Maintain and improve the physical plant in a manner consistent with the quality of the educational program.

Support the college's mission by providing quality services that foster a safe and healthy campus environment: develop and maintain attractive, functional, and efficient facilities, and meet specific academic and business needs in a manner consistent with responsible fiscal and environmental stewardship.

The mission statement should answer the questions who, what, why, and how. Some additional examples of mission statements follow.

The mission of the physical plant department is to provide a safe, healthy environment that will provide the support that our students need to meet the rigorous educational requirements established by the college in its educational mission.

Provide a safe, well-maintained facility that focuses on reliability, strength, and compassion. Maintain an open line of communications with the students and staff.

To provide our community with an environment that is safe, secure, and attractive, and contributes to the attainment of the educational mission of the college.

Provide women with a high quality, safe educational experience in liberal arts curriculum.

The facilities department is committed to quality and competitive service. Our mission is to anticipate and provide the physical environment that enables the college community to achieve its objectives in its educational mission.

These statements provide answers to the questions we asked earlier about the role of the facilities department in the institutional setting. They help everyone in the department to focus on what the facilities organization is and does. The next element of the plan should be a statement of vision for the future.

Developing a Department Vision

Visioning looks at the future with a sense of what we want to do or be in a couple of years. What is our vision for the future? The goals may not be attainable now, but they should be realistic. Achieving the ability to jump tall buildings in a single bound can never be accomplished; however, to say that "we want to have the best, most well-trained team in the institution" is attainable.

Some examples of vision statements follow:

To be one of the best college or university facilities operations by offering high quality services with good value while ensuring the financial stability of the organization.

Or more specifically:

In five years the department will have completely integrated its information systems with the college's system so that all of our customers can determine the status of their request by accessing the database.

Values

Values are a critical part of the plan because they are the structural basis of a department. The team should examine and define the department's collective values. Without commitment to all of the components, service to customers is disjointed and inconsistent. Some value statements are:

How we accomplish our mission is as important as the mission itself. Fundamental to the physical plant department's success are these basic values....Our people are the source of our strength. They provide our reputation and vitality. Involvement and teamwork are our core human values. Our customers are our most important asset. Our service is the end result of our efforts. As our services are viewed, so we are viewed. Our trust is the effective use of the college's investment in the physical plant.

Individual leadership, innovation, the pursuit of excellence, and personal integrity and accountability are cornerstones supported by new technologies that improve service performance and product delivery. An open environment produces teamwork, diversity, customer service, communications, continuous quality improvement and performance, and a workforce that contributes toward the success of the overall organization.

A Stakeholder Analysis

As part of the organizational profile the team must differentiate between the department's customers and its stakeholders. Doing so will enable the team to then identify the needs of each constituent group.

Stakeholders are those groups who have an interest in the mission of the department. An analysis of who the stakeholders are will sharpen our ability to examine critically our strengths, weaknesses, opportunities, and threats. Some of the stakeholders in a higher education facilities environment are

- **Students**—They are the group to which the college has committed its resources. They use the residence halls and educational facilities to achieve the results that the college or university has established in its educational mission statement. They are also the future alumni.

- **Parents**—Those who pay the tuition, which makes the mission possible.

- **Board of directors or trustees**—They have the fiduciary responsibility for the college operation and are interested in the goals presented above.
- **Faculty**—The people who provide the central resource of knowledge for the students. They are vital to fulfilling the institution's mission of education.
- **Staff**—This group provides support for the institution so that the mission can be accomplished in concert with the efforts expended by the faculty.
- **President and administrative leaders**—They provide the leadership and vision for the institution.
- **Alumni**—An important constituent group that provides a substantial contribution to the annual fund or the endowment of the college or university. They view the college from two perspectives: as former students, with all of the perceptions they may have had about our facilities; and as returning visitors taking pride in the organization that created new friendships and careers.
- **Outside suppliers**—Those firms that we depend on to provide the material and services we need to keep the operation moving, to meet the mission of the college or university.
- **State legislature**—For state institutions, this body provides the funding and regulation for the university.

Define the importance of each group to the physical plant department, identifying their needs and the ways they might support or resist the department. Try also to define how each of them would assess the performance of the department. At some point, it is wise to bring in some of the important representatives of the stakeholders and ask what their performance criteria are. We should ask ourselves, what makes us unique in their perception?

When the stakeholder assessment is complete and the needs assessment has been reviewed by the planning team, the department's mission statement should be reviewed to determine if it meets the needs of the primary stakeholders. Any inconsistencies between the needs and the mission should be addressed.

Strategic Goals

The next step in the process is to identify some strategic goals. Some possible goals and objectives for a facilities department are

- To provide first-class service to the customers on the campus.
- To decrease the energy cost by some percentage over the next year.
- To give all students access to computer registration within the next three years.
- To implement a total quality management program in the next five years.
- To have campus-wide scheduling and communications of all events and maintenance activities.
- Improve the relationship with the local government and also the college community.
- Make the services more cost effective.
- Develop a marketing strategy for the department by providing key information to the institutional leadership.

The strategic goals developed by the team will be used in evaluating the department's strengths, weaknesses, opportunities, and threats, a process known as SWOT analysis. Only after establishing these goals can we examine how our department's SWOT affects its ability to attain its goals. The SWOT will allow us to see our shortcomings and obstacles. The results are used to develop policies and procedures that maximize efficiency while maintaining and enhancing the integrity of the college or university. Examples of strategic goals include the following:

Increase productivity through employee development and education, use continuous quality improvement techniques, use new technologies better, rightsize, reengineer, and draw on the talent and expertise of all employees.

Develop operational and fiscal plans to fulfill the college or university's responsibility for the preservation of the environment.

Enhance the opportunities for students to utilize facilities and services for laboratory and educational experiences.

*Provide hospitality, recreation, meeting, and support services for
faculty, staff, students, guests, alumni, and friends of the college
or university.*

One of the most effective methods for coming up with strategic goals is by brainstorming. In order for the brainstorming
session to be productive, the following guidelines are suggested:

1. Select a facilitator.
2. Select the team.
3. Select an area, on or off campus, that will provide privacy
   and permit ideas to flow freely.
4. Focus on a single question or issue at a time.
5. Record all the ideas on a flip chart.
6. The team should select the best five or six ideas by voting
   for those they feel are best for the department.
7. Record the ideas with the largest number of votes on a new
   sheet of paper.
8. Arrange the ideas according to their perceived priority.

After the ideas are in the order that the team approves,
further discussion of priorities should take place. At the com-
pletion of the session, the charts can be typed and distributed
to the entire group.

Bear in mind that brainstorming will produce ideas based on
the perceived needs of the team members present at the time.
As staff changes, the list of ideas will too. Remain committed
to the objective of finding the several important ideas that
accurately reflect the department's assessment.

Strengths, Weaknesses, Opportunities, and Threats Evaluation

The SWOT evaluation or strategic analysis is an in-depth
examination of the internal and external factors that will have
a potential impact on the department in the future. It represents the database of those factors that have been determined
to be important for developing the strategic plan. It should look
at and consider all of the forces that affect the department, and
the factors the department must consider while implementing
the strategic plan. The analysis will also systematize the envi-

ronmental evaluation process, and it will allow a forum for expressing divergent views about the changes taking place within and outside of the department or institution.

SWOT analysis also plays an important role indeveloping the financial plan later. Financial constraints and opportunities will be revealed in the process, and these will be vital to both the financial and strategic plans.

Gathering the items for analysis might begin with simply stating an issue based on some observations and soliciting suggestions as to how to approach the problem. Some topic ideas that might be discussed during a SWOT evaluation include

- Where do our operations stand as compared with other facilities operations?
- What are some unfunded mandates affecting the department or the institution?
- What current federal, state, or local regulations affect facilities operations?
- Examine training costs both for staff enhancement and regulatory compliance.
- Examine departmental funding shortfalls, departmental processes, work order management, customer service, contracted services, bidding processes for pricing, service improvements.

Try to keep everything as simple as possible. An overly elaborate process tends to constrain strategic thinking. A simple method that may be used to gather ideas is the "snow card" technique. Give everyone a blank card on which they can anonymously write their ideas. Members of the team who are unable to verbalize their ideas may find it easier to articulate them on paper. The cards are then collected and the ideas recorded. No matter what method is used for brainstorming, however, encourage the team to consider external events and incorporate these facts in their thinking.

Once the lists are consolidated, the team should attempt to order the items by priority or as part of a schedule for the future. Often, patterns will appear in the list that suggest a priority, even if it was not part of the intent.

Repeat or at least review the categories later to determine if they are still issues of concern in the future. These reevaluations should be done on a regular basis as the strategic plan develops and should continue after the plan has been implemented.

You might also consider, as part of the criteria for the assessment of SWOT, a description of the issue, why it is a strategic issue, and some discussion of what will happen if the issue is not resolved. Keep in mind that the strategic plan will suggest a number of positive factors that are inherent in the operation.

After the list of strategic issues has been developed, each issue should be evaluated to determine its importance to developing the strategic plan. Examine the issues in terms of what the department is doing well and not so well. What factors influence the department's performance? Look at the internal and external factors that can help and hinder the department's progress toward its stated strategic goals. Here is an example of a SWOT analysis.

Internal strengths of the facilities department:
- The departmental personnel are well-trained, skilled, dedicated, and motivated.
- Plant staff, senior level management, and the board of directors are committed to quality facilities.
- The campus has in place an excellent internal work order and accounting computer system and a superior computerized energy management system.
- A safe and well-equipped physical environment is provided for the staff.
- There is no deferred maintenance.

External strengths:
- We have a committed cadre of contractors who provide high-level services to the college.
- Our suppliers work with the college to provide material deliveries that are on time, in the quantities we need, and at the best price available.
- We enjoy a good collaborative relationship with other colleges and universities in the area and country.

Internal weaknesses:
- A decreasing amount of available funding to adequately complete the assigned tasks and the stated mission of the department.
- There are a number of historical buildings on the campus that require a higher than average commitment of resources.
- We have a limited staff to do the job. We are in the process of downsizing the operation.
- There is a reduced financial base created by a shrinking student population.
- A crumbling infrastructure that requires large infusions of capital to initiate repairs or replacement.

External weaknesses:
- There are a limited number of suppliers of services and materials in the area, which leads to long lead times for parts and extra expenses for the delivery of services.

Internal opportunities:
- An accurate audit of the facility has been performed and it sets the direction for the future.
- A long-range plan for construction projects has been identified and has support from the senior staff and the board of directors.
- All of the safety and environmental issues have been identified and included in the long-range plan for the institution.

External opportunities:
- The support from local and state authorities is good, and work with the institution to support the needs of the community and the institution.

Internal threats:
- Changes in customer expectations after budgeting process is completed.
- A reduction in the reimbursable income available to do the work required.

- Poor estimating procedures that fail to define the scope of the work prior to the start of construction.
- New environmental regulations from the federal and state government.
- New OSHA standards will increase the expenditures for safety equipment.

External threats:
- Federal, state, and local unfunded mandates, ADA, OSHA, EPA, and DER regulations.
- Governmental interference, challenges to tax-exempt status.
- Changes in building codes while in the construction stage. More than one building code or agency applicable for the project.

Figure 1 represents a matrix that can be used to test the validity of strategic issues as they are determined by the planning team. You can see that strategic issues are defined as those that have a great impact on the campus, involve many departments, and require substantial amounts of time and money.

Recapping, the efforts to date in the strategic planning process include

1. The departmental leadership has identified the need to create strategic plan and set some broad goals for the department.

2. A team has reviewed the institutional mission statement and created a departmental statement that supports that statement.

3. That team or another has developed a series of goals, visions, and value statements, after which the key strategic issues facing the department will be articulated and recorded.

The Financial Plan

A strategic plan will, after identifying all of the key issues facing the department over the next few years, lead to the development

Figure 1.
Matrix for evaluating strategic issues.

	Operations ⟶		Strategic
1. When will the strategic issues or opportunities confront you?	now	next year	3 or more years
2. How broad an impact will the issue have on your department?	a single trade unit	several trade units	the entire department
3. How large is your department's financial risk/financial opportunity?	minor—10% of budget	Moderate—25% of budget	major—more than 25% of budget
4. Will strategies for issue resolution likely require			
a. development of new service goals?	no	small	yes
b. significant changes in department funding?	no	small	yes
c. significant changes in facilities?	no	small	yes
d. significant changes in staff?	no	small	yes
5. How easy will it be to define some approach to resolve the issue?	obvious & ready to go	broad definition	wide open, anything goes
6. What is the lowest level of management that can decide how to deal with this issue?	trade foremen	line supervisor	department head and senior level management
7. What will happen if the issue is not resolved in some way?	inconvenience or inefficiency	significant service disruption	major down time for major portions of campus
8. How many sub-units or other departments are affected by the decision?	one	two or three	four or more
9. If other departments are involved, can the problem be solved without departmental chairs?	yes	it is likely but may be problematic	department chairs probably involved
10. How sensitive is this issue?	not serious	somewhat touchy	explosive and has profound impact on campus

*This chart is based on a model used by Hennepin county, Minnesota in 1983. It is designed to look at the implications of each item in the strategic plan, testing if the item is operation or strategic in nature. The broader the issue, the more strategic in scope.

of a comprehensive financial document. That document can be used to support a phased program for the facilities department and should include all of the program elements applicable to the entire college or university. The strategic plan, especially the results of the SWOT analysis, can also serve as the beginning of a long-range financial plan and then an operations budget when the elements are distributed over an appropriate time period. Other important components in the development of a financial plan are discussed below.

Facilities Audits

A major component of any strategic plan is a complete facilities audit to assess the condition of the institution's facilities. An initial audit will establish a baseline for the institution, and follow-up audits will fine-tune the data and track any changes. Subsequent comprehensive audits may not have to be performed for several years. In some cases, the frequency of the audit of particular buildings may depend on type and use rate. In other cases, a change in the frequency of breakdowns may indicate a need to adjust the frequency of the audit.

Master Planning

An institution's master plan should reflect the immediate and long-term goals for the campus. The process should include a series of consensus discussions with various constituent groups within the campus community. Discussions should focus on pedestrian flow, automobile movement and parking, academic program requirements, administrative and support spaces, and residence halls. Infrastructure and landscape improvements must also be included. The master plan is a dynamic document, subject to minor changes from time to time, but it charts the course for the future.

Regulatory Compliance

Regulations and their impact on the financial operations are an important part of our future financial planning. Changes to laws and regulations make periodic reviews an ongoing necessity for planning. Institutional compliance for some regulations can be staged, while others require more immediate action. If a planned phase-in can be accomplished and still meet lawful requirements, then timelines can be incorporated into the long-range plan.

Infrastructure Improvements

Facilities audits might not include a review of infrastructure changes that are predictive: underground steam, electrical, communications, water, and sewer lines all have a finite lifetime. While engineering studies are important and provide credibility to any survey, technical discussions are not interesting to the senior leadership; therefore, information provided should relate to the mission and goals of the college or university.

Energy Audits

An energy audit is a survey of the campus buildings to determine energy consumption patterns. An audit should look at the types of construction, HVAC systems, hours of operation, and equipment-connected loads. This data is then compared with the utility bills for the previous year.

Based on the profiles calculated, various utility areas can be targeted for reductions. Oftentimes it is possible to obtain permission to divert funds from the utility budget line to energy reduction efforts and thus save in energy costs.

Risk Management

Does risk management enter into a strategic financial plan? Below are just a few examples of problems we have to at least be aware of for the future. A problem with any one of these can open the institution to lawsuits and potential loss or severe escalation of insurance costs.

- Motor vehicle accidents
- Falls in the workplace
- Fires
- Inhalation and ingestion of objects (indoor air quality)
- Accidental poisoning from gases and vapors, solids, and liquids.
- Electrocution
- Natural disasters: tornadoes, floods, lightning, snow, and hurricanes. Initiate disaster planning programs.
- Inadequate physical barriers

- Employment practices and forms that might lead to litigation.

Funding the Financial Plan

Having completed a comprehensive financial plan for the future of our institution's facility and created a long list of strategic objectives, plans have to be made to fund the process. APPA and NACUBO have suggested that an institution should set aside from two to five percent of the replacement value of the facilities each year to fund its programs. For many institutions, that amount of money is not available. Institutions are struggling with budgets for operations. While the funding for these projects is important, the annual operating budget is critical for the continued operation for all departments.

Following are suggestions for ways to accomplish the goals established in a financial plan. These are only a few possible approaches, and they will not provide complete funding, but they are a start.

Strategic Outsourcing

We all outsource to some degree. In the past it was called subcontracting for services. Small colleges have been doing it for years to augment permanent staff and to reduce costs. Larger universities are also now doing the same thing. As part of the strategic planning process it is important to list all of the outsourcing efforts your college or university has made to date.

Benchmarking with Other Facilities Departments

Benchmarking is used by many institutions as a way to draw direct comparisons with other departments of similar size and character. Comparing data on facilities, number of employees, pay rates, utility costs, and number of students can reflect how effectively we are doing the job. The APPA *Comparative Costs and Staffing Report* is one source of such data.

Suggestions for the benchmarking process follow:

1. Determine what areas you want to benchmark.

2. Determine comparable institutions.

3. Make the collection process as easy as possible and then collect the data.

4. Based on the survey data, determine where your current performance ranks.

5. Project some future performance levels.

6. Make sure that everyone understands the methodology employed in the process.

7. Let everyone know about the results.

8. Discuss the results of the highest performers and compare your processes to see if you can adapt their methodologies to emulate their results. For example, if someone records energy costs of 50 cents per square foot, and your cost is 90 cents per square foot, what are they doing differently?

9. Establish some new goals based on comparisons.

10. Implement some specific actions based on goals established and be sure to track any changes.

11. Fine-tune the system after it has been in operation for a time.

12. Review the process and resurvey after an appropriate period of time to confirmthat your actions are progressing toward your goals.

Conclusion

One institution responding to the rightsizing survey recommended a strategy they were using: do nothing to a building on campus. Their intent was to use it until it literally fell apart and then close it. This approach is radical, but they were unable to get any additional funding.

While during difficult times this approach might seem tempting, I contend we must be creative and look within our department for the funding. Programs such as strategic outsourcing, energy reductions, third-party financing, and leasing, can enable us to do capital reconstruction without demanding monies from the traditional sources.

We have to become salespeople, we have to sell the facilities end of the academic mission of our colleges and universities. And all of our efforts must focus on how our plans help meet the institutional mission. We as facilities managers have to compete with all of the other departments on our campuses for funds. To do this, we must uphold the mission and sell not the preservation of buildings, but the impact these buildings and their condition have on college or university programs.

I am convinced that we and our institutions will have to radically change our thinking in the future. Institutional thinking will have to be replaced by business thinking. Every action we take in the future will have to be based on sound business practices. Unless we are able to make this change, we will follow in the footsteps of the dinosaurs. Our operations and, indeed, the institutions that have served as a model for the rest of the world will disappear, replaced by firms capable of vision and leadership.

Acknowledgments

My thanks to Norman Bedell, Pennsylvania State University, for the information he provided on strategic planning at Penn State for facilities departments, and to Donald Mackel, University of New Mexico, for allowing me to read the strategic plan developed for the facilities department at his university.

Bibliography

American School and University. "Annual Maintenance and Operations Cost Study." *American School & University,* annually.

Anfuso, D. "Recruitment by the Numbers." *Personnel Journal,* vol. 72, no. 2, December 1993.

APPA: The Association of Higher Education Facilities Officers. *Comparative Costs and Staffing Report for College and University Facilities.* Alexandria, Virginia: APPA, biennial.

———. *Contracting for Facilities Services.* (Critical Issues in Facilities Management series, no. 9.) Alexandria, Virginia: APPA, 1994.

———. *The Energy Management Workbook.* Alexandria, Virginia: APPA, 1994.

———. *Facilities Stewardship in the 1990s.* Alexandria, Virginia: APPA, 1991.

———. *Physical Plant Job Descriptions.* Alexandria, Virginia: APPA, 1991.

———. *Management Basics.* (Critical Issues in Facilities Management series, no. 5.) Alexandria, Virginia: APPA, 1990.

Bell, Howard W. Jr., and Nancy J. Hanseman. "Alphabet Soup of Management Tools: Cincinnati's ASEP Process Resembles TQM, CQI, and QPS." *Business Officer,* vol. 27, no. 7, January 1994.

Bell, Chip R. *Customers as Partners.* San Francisco, Virginia: Berrett-Koehler, 1994.

Beltrametti, Monica. "Computing Services Planning, Downsizing, and Organization at the University of Alberta." *CAUSE/EFFECT,* vol. 16, no. 3, Fall 1993.

Boyer, Ernest L. *College: The Undergraduate Experience in America.* New York: Harper & Row, 1987.

Braver, Roger L. *Facilities Planning.* American Management Association, 1986.

Bryson, John M. *Strategic Planning for Public & Non-Profit Organizations: A Guide to Strengthening and and Sustaining Organizational Achievement.* San Francisco: Jossey-Bass Publishers, 1988.

Burton, Jennus L. "Hopping Out of the Swamp: Management of Change in a Downsizing Environment." *Business Officer,* vol. 26, no. 8, February 1993.

Butterfield, Barbara S., and Susan Wolfe. "Downsizing without Discriminating against Minorities and Women." *CUPA Journal,* vol. 44, no. 2, Summer 1993.

Camp, R. *Benchmarking.* Milwaukee, Wisconsin: ASQC Quality Press, 1989.

Clagett, Craig A. *No Pain, No Gain: How One College Emerged Stronger from the Fiscal Crisis.* Largo, Maryland: Prince George's Community College, 1993.

Clark, C. V. "Downsizing Trounces Diversity." *Black Enterprise,* vol. 24, no. 7, February 1994.

Carnegie Foundation for the Advancement of Teaching. "How Do Students Choose a College?" *Change,* January/February 1986.

Covey, Stephen R. *The 7 Habits of Highly Effective People: Restoring the Character Ethic.* New York: Simon & Schuster, 1989.

Council of Higher Education Management Associations (CHEMA). *Contract Management or Self-Operation: A Decision-Making Guide for Higher Education.* Alexandria, Virginia: APPA for the Council of Higher Education Management Associations, 1993.

Cross, M., ed. *Managing Workforce Reduction.* New York: Praeger, 1985.

Daigneau, William A. "The Physical Plant: Asset or Liability?" *Business Officer,* vol. 27, no. 9, March 1994.

Dawson, Bradley L. "The Incredible Shrinking Institution: A Five-Component Downsizing Model." *Business Officer,* vol. 25, no. 1, July 1991.

Deal, Terrence E., and William A. Jenkins. "Spotlighting Backstage Employees." *Business Officer,* vol. 27, no. 9, March 1994.

Dews, Ted. "Process or Product? Today's Resource Allocation Dilemma." In *Proceedings of the 81st Annual Meeting.* Alexandria, Virginia: APPA, 1994.

Dillow, Rex O., ed. *Facilities Management: A Manual for Plant Administration,* 2nd ed. Alexandria, Virginia: APPA, 1989.

Dougherty, Jennifer, et al. *Business Process Redesign for Higher Education.* Washington, D.C.: National Association of College of Unviersity Business Officers, 1994.

Dudley, Jack C., ed. *Custodial Staffing Guidelines for Educational Facilities.* Alexandria, Virginia: APPA, 1992.

Dudley, Jack C., and Robert A. Getz. "The APPA Custodial Staffing Guidelines After a Year at Work: Six Case Studies." In *Proceedings of the 80th Annual Meeting.* Alexandria, Virginia: APPA, 1993.

Eisen, R. "Devising a Layoff Contingency Plan." *HR Magazine,* vol. 38, no. 6, June 1993.

Fagiano, D. "The Downside of Downsizing." *Security Management,* vol. 36, no. 10, October 1992.

Gardner, Catherine, et al. "Stanford and the Railroad: Case Studies of Cost Cutting." *Change,* vol. 22, no. 6, November/December 1990.

Gardner, James R., Robert Rachlin, and H. W. Allen Sweeny, eds. *Handbook of Strategic Planning.* New York: Wiley Interscience Publications, 1986.

Getz, Robert A. "Handling Layoffs with Compassion and Dignity." In *Proceedings of the 79th Annual Meeting.* Alexandria, Virginia: APPA, 1992.

Glazner, Steve, ed. *Facilities Manager.* Theme issue on customer service, Summer 1994.

——. *Facilities Manager.* Theme issue on leadership, Winter 1995.

Hammer, Michael, and James Champy. *Reengineering the Corporation: A Manifesto for Business Revolution.* New York: Harper Business, 1993.

Heenan, D. O. "The Right Way to Downsize." *Journal of Business Strategy,* vol. 12, no. 5, September/October 1991.

Hendricks, C. F. *The Rightsizing Remedy.* Homewood, Illinois: Society for Human Resource Management and Business One Irwin, 1992.

Henkoff, R. "Getting Beyond Downsizing." *Fortune,* vol, 129, no. 1, January 10, 1994.

"HR Paints a Bleak Portrait of Downsizing Survivors." *HR Focus,* vol. 70, no. 5, May 1993.

Hughes, K. Scott, and Daryl Conner, eds. *Managing Change in Higher Education: Preparing for the 21st Century.* Washington, D.C.: Colllege and University Personnel Association, 1989.

Kaiser, Harvey H. "Rightsizing/Downsizing: The Role of Facilities Management." In *Practical Approaches to Rightsizing.* Washington,

D.C.: National Association of College and University Business Officers, 1992.

——. "Rightsizing Through Restructuring: A Higher Education Challenge." *Facilities Manager,* Fall 1994.

Klee, Frederick L. "Report from the Rightsizing Task Force." *Facilities Manager,* Spring 1994.

——. "Roundtable Roundup: Rightsizing." *Facilities Manager,* Fall 1994.

Lawlor, Patrick J. "Downsizing Creatively: Doing More for Less." In *Proceedings of the 79th Annual Meeting.* Alexamdria, Virginia: APPA, 1992.

Lawrence, A. T., and B. S. Mittman. "Downsizing on the Upswing." *Personnel,* vol. 68, no. 2, February 1991.

Larkey, Linda Kathryn. "Perceptions of Discrimination During Downsizing." *Management Communication Quarterly,* vol. 7, no. 2, November 1993.

Lively, K. "State Colleges Grapple with Tough Decisions on How to 'Downsize.'" *Chronicle of Higher Education,* vol. 39, no. 22, February 3, 1993.

Long, Norma R. "Anatomy of Continuing Education Downsizing." *Journal of Continuing Higher Education,* vol. 41, no. 3, Fall 1993.

Loomis, C. J. "Dinosaurs." *Fortune,* May 3, 1993.

National Association of College and University Business Officers (NACUBO). *Practical Approaches to Rightsizing.* Washington, D.C.: NACUBO, 1992.

Norman, Colin. "Downsizing at the University of Michigan." *Science,* vol. 220, no. 4594, April 15, 1983.

Pastin, Mark. "Power, Influence, and Survival in Difficult Times." *Facilities Manager,* Fall 1992.

Peters, Thomas. *Thriving on Chaos.* New York: Harper & Row, 1987.

Raisman, Neal A. "Plan for Change Before Someone Else Plans it for You." *Trusteeship,* vol. 2, no. 4, July/August 1994.

Reinhard, Bill. "The Federal Challenge to Our Community Colleges." *Journal of Career Planning and Employment,* vol. 54, no. 4, May 30, 1994.

Reynolds, Gary L., ed. *Building Quality: TQM for Campus Facilities Managers.* Alexandria, Virginia: APPA, 1994.

Rushan, C. "Productivity or Quality? In Search of Higher Education's Yellow Brick Road." *Business Officer,* vol. 25, no. 10, April 1992.

Schaffer, Susan M. "Reformation Comes to the University." *Journal of Higher Education Management,* vol. 8, no. 1, Fall 1992.

Sexton, William P. "Merging Your Goals for Excellence with the Institution's Mission." *Facilities Manager,* Winter 1989.

Smith, Samuel H. "Educational Leadership: The Role of Facilities in Educational Excellence." *Facilities Manager,* Fall 1992.

Smith, Hoke L. "The Incredible Shrinking College: Downsizing as Positive Planning." *Educational Record,* vol. 67, no. 2-3, Spring/Summer 1986.

Steiner, George A. *Strategic Planning: What Every Manager Must Know.* New York: The Free Press, 1979.

Swistock, J.R., and Michael P. Onder. "Building a Base for Change." In *Proceedings of the 79th Annual Meeting.* Alexandria, Virginia: APPA, 1992.

Tichey, Noel M., and Stratford Sherman. *Control Your Own Destiny or Someone Else Will.* New York: Doubleday/Currency, 1993.

Weinstein, Laurence A. *Moving a Battleship with Your Bare Hands: Governing a University System.* Madison, Wisconsin: Magna Publications, 1993.

Appendix: Rightsizing Survey Responses

Total responses = **388**

1. Experienced budget reductions in at least 1 of the last 5 years. **106**

2. Experienced budget reductions in at least 1 of the last 5 years AND anticipate additional reductions during the next 2 years. **168**

3. Experienced a level budget for at least 1 of the last 3 years. **45**

4. Experienced no budget reductions during the last 3 years. **18**

5. Experienced no budget reductions during the last 3 years BUT do anticipate budget cuts during at least 1 of the next 2 years. **13**

6. Experienced a budget increase in at least 1 of the last 3 years. **20**

7. Experienced a budget increase in at least 1 of the last 3 years AND anticipate an increase during at least 1 of the next 2 years. **38**

8. None of the above. **44**

[No question 9 on survey.]

10. Indicate range of cumulative budget and staff reductions.

Budget		**Staff**	
44	Less than 2 percent	89	1 to 5 percent
90	3 to 5 percent	64	5 to 10 percent
39	6 to 9 percent	26	10 to 15 percent
82	10 percent or higher	39	Above 15 percent

11. Provide percentage of personnel reductions in each area:

Custodial	**13.40**	Trades (mechanical/electrical/etc.)	**11.30**
Grounds	**15.24**	Painting	**30.08**

12. What has been the number of full-time unfilled plant positions since
    reductions first were imposed?   **19.1**

a.   Has the number of part-time positions
     Increased **75**   Decreased **62**   Remained constant **118**

     Indicate reasons for reductions (Number of "yes" responses.)

     Mandated due to reduced state funding   **155**

     Physical plant reductions due to increased funding of
     other departments.   **63**

     Reduced student enrollment, tuition fees, and etc.   **81**

     Revision of our insitution's academic mission   **155**

     Others   **42**

13. Indicate any other departments at your institution that have had the
     same or greater percentage reductions as facilities.

     Academic **92**   Student Life **60**

     Residential Life **54**   Other Administrative Areas **157**

14. Using a scale of 1-5, indicate all groups that were involved in the
    retrenchment/restructuring process and indicate their support or resis-
    tance.

    1=Highest level   5=Lowest level

Group	Support	S-Count	Resistance	R-Count
President	1.9	216	3.9	38
Your Boss	1.8	221	3.7	46
Faculty	2.9	121	3.0	108
Students	3.2	89	3.2	82
Trustees	2.2	156	3.7	33
Physical Plant Staff	2.5	159	2.9	96
University Community	2.9	109	3.2	70
Cost Containment Committee	2.4	85	3.7	25

15. Rank on a scale of 1 to 5 all areas where adjustments have been
    made due to retrenchment/restructuring?

    1=Highest level of adjustments 5=Lowest level of adjustments

	Average Rank	Total Score
Early retirement of staff	**3.2**	**204**
Unfilled staff positions	**1.6**	**241**

Forced reduction of staff	2.9	212
Privatization of activities	3.9	189
Purchasing fewer equipment	2.5	237
Purchasing less supplies	2.8	228
Elimination of travel & training	2.8	225
Reduction of hours in the work week	4.5	169
Reduced staff benefits	4.1	177
Reduced or freeze in current staff wages	2.7	217
Reduced levels of service	2.9	233

16. The financial retrenchment/restructuring at our institution has caused the following affect on academic programs. (Number of "yes" responses.)

Minor changes	161
Major changes	36
No changes	77

17. The long-term impact on the condition of facilities at our institution, due to budget reductions is expected to: (Number of "yes" responses.)

Improve	33
Decline	164
Remain the same	79

18. Does the physical plant department at your institution have the ability to interchange funding amounts between budget categories?
Yes   346

19. Does the physical plant department at your institution have the ability to carryover unexpended funds into the next fiscal year?
Yes   127

20. If an unbudgeted "critical emergency breakdown" occurs, are funds available from sources other than the operating budget?
Yes   313

21. Indicate the areas within your institution that have a strategic plan:

Institution as a whole	284
Academic departments	100
Individual support areas	83

Facilities department   **166**

22. Has the strategic plan been implemented? ("Yes" responses.)   **247**

23. Were you, as physical plant director involved in the development of
the strategic plan? ("Yes" responses.)   **259**

24. Were reductions/restructuring done in the context of the strategic plan?

Yes   **129**

25. OMITTED

26. Total gross square feet maintained by operations & maintenance budget.

Average   **2,458,255**

27. Total number of physical plant employees

Average   **156**

28. Are some of your operations funded by reimbursable funds?

Yes   **231**

29. Does your institution have:

a) Division I Athletic Program   **127**

b) Hospital/Medical Facility   **80**

c) Research Funding   **205**